Volume one - birth to eighteen years

Frank Samuel Foweraker

Born in 1926 in the East End of London to a working-class family at the outset of the great depression was not an auspicious start ...
'My Life' is my memories from as young as I can remember, in my own words.

My intention was just to let my children, grandchildren, great-grandchildren - and any more to come, know a bit about where they came from, but in doing so it seems I have included a lot of what is considered first-hand recollections of social history.

This book takes me up until I was eighteen, volume two is written and, now at 90, I continue to write ...

FRANK
My Life

Volume one - birth to eighteen years

Frank Samuel Foweraker

Copyright © 2016 by Frank S Foweraker
ISBN: 978-1-909936-90-4

Frank S Foweraker has asserted his right under the Copyright, Designs and Patents Act 1988 to be identified as the author of this work

All rights reserved. This book or any portion thereof may not be reproduced or used in any manner whatsoever without the express written permission of the publisher except for the use of brief quotations in a book review.

Paperback Edition 2016 Pendown Publishing
Cornwall, United Kingdom

Set in 12pt Gentium BB

Printed by Lightning Source

www.pendownpublishing.co.uk

Cover: NJM designs

For my descendants

*And dedicated to Win Foweraker
the love of my life and wife since 1953*

FRANK
My Life

Volume one - birth to eighteen years

Frank Samuel FOWERAKER

FRANK My Life
Frank Samuel Foweraker
Volume one - birth to eighteen years

chapters

1	the beginning
2	home again
3	times at Taw Green Mill
4	cripple school
5	at Woolmore Street School
6	the start of my plan
7	foot notes
8	beating the bullies
9	new additions
10	boys' camp
11	running the pro-house
12	of mice and teachers
13	the church and decisions
14	back to boys' camp
15	Uncle George's prediction
16	evacuation part one
17	evacuation two – pillar to post
18	home and work
19	bombing raids
20	down to Davoncourt

(Where photographs have been included they are generally at the end of the relevant chapter)

chapters

21	learning the farming ropes
22	of moles and cones
23	Devon snow
24	to be a farmer's boy
25	calves and lambs
26	rams, stallions and slag
27	threshers and shearers
28	bikes and emergencies
29	haymaking, harvest and disputes
30	Bess!!
31	sheep and 'mother'
32	pony and tractor
33	rams, cards and a foal
34	a bit of a knock
35	a whole new start
36	cider, compass and ATC
37	shooting, scythe and Yanks
38	toothache, enemies and dances
39	a prediction, a rabbit and arsenic
40	barrier, haircut - and the letter

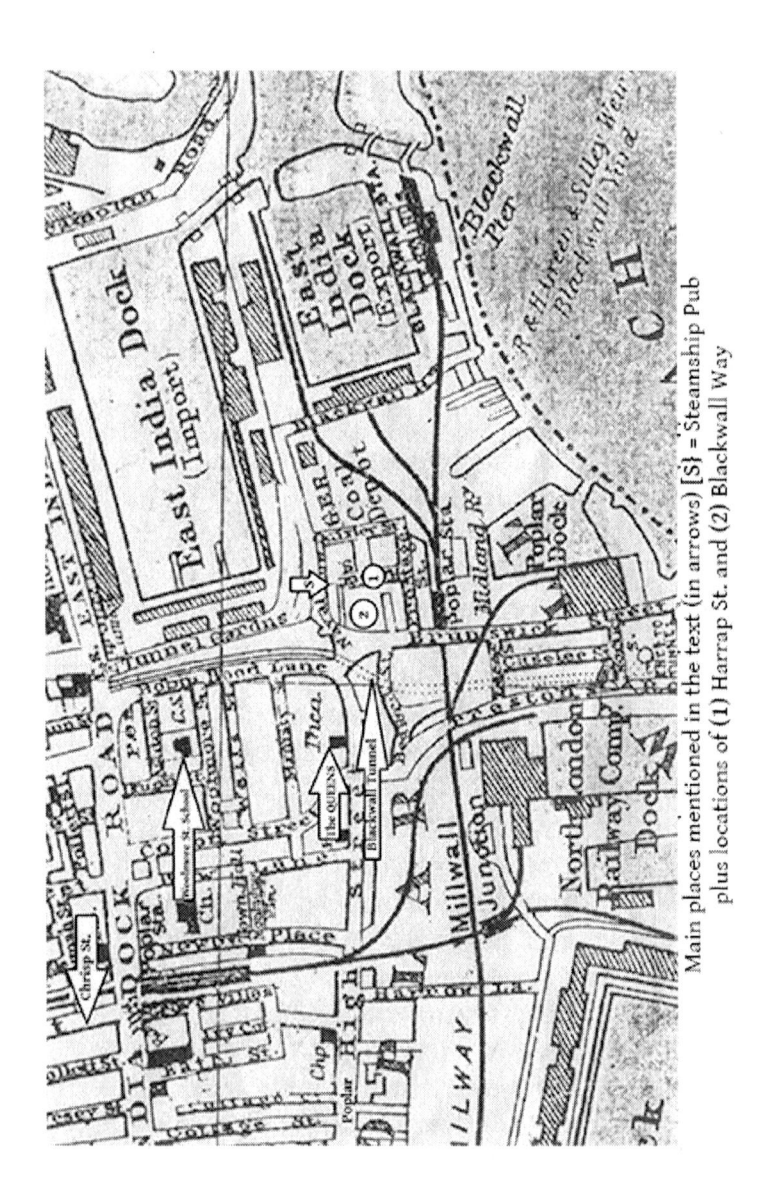

Main places mentioned in the text (in arrows) [S] = Steamship Pub
plus locations of (1) Harrap St. and (2) Blackwall Way

Chapter 1   the beginning

I was born on 12th June, 1926, in Harrap Street, Poplar, in the East End of London, the first child of my parents and what follows in this first chapter is what I was told by my parents as well as memories that nobody could have told me - because I was alone in hospital from the age of eighteen months until the age of four years.

A bit of background first - the state of the economy was low and, though my father had a job, the wage was poor as there were a lot of unemployed. It was a struggle to make ends meet. Consequently they were in a bad nutritional state already, and then employers wanted to cut wages by a shilling a week.

The miners called a national strike and evidently all the small employers locked their workers out, so my father lost the little income he had. Mum and Dad went to the relief office to ask for a bread voucher, and the officer said, 'Why don't you send your wife out to work?' and Dad said she was not in a condition to work. The officer said, 'Bring her in and let's have a look at her – is she crippled or something?' (Nobody made mention of pregnancy in those days). When he saw Mum, he said, 'That's not my fault, and if you can't feed your wife, you should keep yourself to yourself, and not come here begging'. Dad grabbed his shirt front and hauled him over the counter. Immediately the copper on duty took Dad to the magistrates who were sitting full-time. Dad explained what had happened, so the magistrate sent for the relief officer who came, full of self-importance, but he was soon told his job was to issue tickets, not pass obnoxious comments on the applicant's condition and to go back and do the job he was paid for. He then told Dad to go back and get the ticket. Dad thanked him and said that if that was what it took to get a loaf of bread he would sooner starve.

The strike was soon over, because of starvation, and the employers took their shilling off the wages, and into this situation I was born. My parents struggled on. The only health service at that time was a scheme called The Panel which only applied to actively working people, not wives or children, so ordinary folk relied on the older women in their street to say what they thought was wrong, and what to do about it. By the time I was 18 months and still could not walk, only crawl dragging my left leg, or stand by a chair with my left leg hanging free, the older women said that I was obviously 'lazy in one leg'. So my parents tightened their belts, found the money, and took me to the GP, who watched me crawl along the floor, then, for one shilling and sixpence, told them that I had a congenitally dislocated hip – just a bald statement – and then left them to get on with it.

Now, to add to their troubles, they knew their first-born was a cripple, doomed to wearing a leg-iron for life, useless and dependant on relief. I think Dad had always belonged to the HSA (Hospital Savings Association), which, for a subscription of about three pence a week, would finance any serious hospital treatment, the full cost of which you paid back in weekly instalments. There was no NHS at that time. I was told he was still paying this back when I was eighteen.

I was taken to Guy's Hospital where they started the attempt to rectify the problem. The ball joint now was above the pelvis and had grown in, so over many weeks it was loosened and, by a system of pulleys and weights, the leg was stretched until the ball was in line with its socket.

My parents said that they couldn't visit much, as they couldn't afford the fares across London, so would walk when the weather permitted. I was only aware of strange faces swimming in and out of my vision.

When the doctors were satisfied with the alignment I was put in a plaster cast from lower ribs to ankles for four months (my parents did visit at this time at least once, for years later I was told I was almost unapproachable because of the stink).

At the end of the four month period the plaster was removed and I was fitted with a corset to keep the hip in place until it became stronger, and I was removed to Shadwell Hospital, where the muscles in my leg were to be exercised and strengthened. Bearing in mind that I had never walked, it must have been very difficult for the nurses.

Life was very confusing for me at the time - apparently during this time I caught all the childhood complaints, and I understand at this time my mother became ill, and visits were even less frequent.

Two things from those last two years at Shadwell remained in my memories – one when we were being washed, the ward-maid would say 'Hold your arm up' and then she would hold your hand and wash your arm down, and then let your hand go to get the towel. If you let your arm drop she would give you a slap and say that she wasn't there to hold your arm up. The other thing that stayed with me was as a recurring nightmare - I used to have miserable earaches at night and cry, and then there was a screeching noise, a stinging slap across the face, then the screeching and a clang! (I will mention this again much later in my story).

My parents said that when they got me home, in 1930, I was so thin I used to sit cross legged in my nappy 'like a little Gandhi', so I suppose that also meant I was not even potty trained. Before I start the next part of my story, I will include a photo taken in 1930. Keeping in mind my parents' description of my condition, by my improved appearance in the photo, it must have been taken later in the year.

I'm told that for quite a while I called mum 'Nurse' and Dad 'that man'. It was all very confusing.

The 'leg-iron' was a brace to keep my hip joint together, formed by a wide leather belt around my waist attached to the 'iron' which extended only down to my upper thigh, where it was held in place by another wide leather belt. This meant that even in shorts it wasn't actually visible. To begin with I needed 'steadying' to stand on the leg, by being held or by leaning against something; a wall, my father's legs - whatever was convenient ... until the muscles strengthened.

One of my earliest photographs

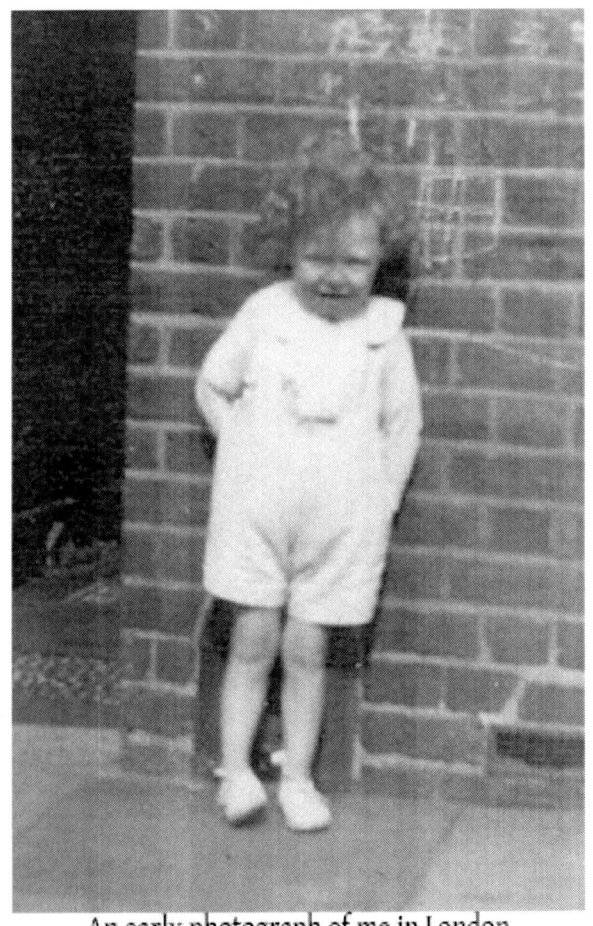

An early photograph of me in London
- probably leaning on the wall for support

Chapter 2 home again

Once I was home, Dad concentrated on getting me on my feet by taking most of my weight and encouraging leg movements in the evenings. Gradually my hip would get to support me. At this stage I went back to Shadwell to be fitted with a boot and small leg-iron.

My parents said that at this time they were ordered to feed me as much fat as possible, and they laughed at it taking the two of them to bath me, as I was so slippery. It took one to hold me while the other one did the bathing, to stop me sliding out of the sink.

Then their finances worsened. In those days, to be a 'landlord' only meant that you were responsible for the rent book, and paying the rent collector the rent for the whole house, which carried the privilege of living downstairs, with the scullery and indoor tap, with the lavatory just outside the back door, and able to sublet the upstairs rooms at slightly more than half rent.

Now for some reason (probably the people upstairs had moved out) Mum and Dad had the whole rent to find, and could not, so we had to move in as sub-tenants in another house, and, of course, it was upstairs, which meant that all the water had to be carried up and down stairs, plus night soil.

One bitter memory from that time was that, with my newfound mobility, I walked around a lot, and one day the 'landlady' screamed up the stairs 'Stop that kid from stomping around'. Mother replied 'I can hardly stop him walking around', but she screamed 'Well, tie him on a chair, or find somewhere else to live'. By now I was about four and a half - the 'landlady' moved, and, as there was more work available, we moved downstairs as 'landlords' again.

One morning, soon after we moved downstairs, Dad walked me and carried me to Newby Place, near All Saints Church, Poplar, and pointed down the 'airy' (the steps to the basement area), and there I saw a lady all in black. This was the nun on duty, one of the Anglican Nuns that were midwives to the people of the East End. He blew down a pipe, and she spoke into the pipe and said, 'Yes?' Dad said, 'Your help is required at fifteen Harrap Street'. She said, 'Thank you', and as Dad walked me home the church bells were ringing – it was Sunday. When Dad put me to bed that night he told me I had a brother. I vaguely remember that all was confusion after - I wasn't taken to see Mum or the brother for ages – it was the custom for the mother and child to stay in bed for a fortnight after birth.

Dad got me up in the mornings and then went to work. Various ladies came in - all were called 'Aunt' - but some were and others were not, and when Dad came home we had our tea. Then, invariably, he took me out to walk up the Poplar High Street, sometimes after dark, as I suppose he had jobs to do first, like cleaning up. As I progressed we went further past all the lit-up shop windows, and gradually increasing the distance, then home and back to bed. His perseverance must have been great, for there was no physiotherapy then.

Around this stage Dad took me by tram to see an old lady. When we arrived at the house we had to go upstairs and, due to the inflexibility of the leg-iron, I had to go up right foot first, then the left to the same step, bump, thump, all the way, and there she was – sitting by the window, all big skirt and lace cap on her head. She watched me walk towards her. 'This is Frank' Dad said, and her reply has haunted me all my life, 'Won't be a lot of good then, will he?' She, I believe, was my Great-grandmother Foweraker.

The walking exercises continued. At one point Dad took to carrying a newspaper, because I had developed a problem. My legs would pain me so much that I could not move. Dad knelt on the paper and rubbed my legs until I could move again. The old ladies 'wisdom' put it down to 'growing pains', but, of course, it was rheumatic fever, and though it passed, it caused permanent damage that was only discovered many years later, which I will refer to at the appropriate time in the story. Gradually my leg grew stronger, with Dad walking me 'Up West' all the time.

I had to go back to Shadwell Hospital from time to time for them to check my progress and eventually they removed the leg-iron and instead I had a pair of boots which came above my ankle, and, as the left leg was not as strong as the right one, a soft leather bag like a sausage, full of lead shot, was tied around my left leg to make it stronger, and this was adjusted from time to time. On each visit Mother had to see the Lady Almoner and pay something.

The walks increased in length until finally we reached the Great Fire of London Memorial; then Dad started me climbing the 127 steps to the top and, over the course of many weeks, I could reach the top, which he'd had in mind all the time.

Some time in this improvement of my hip joint and leg muscles, Mum and Dad took me to Regent's Park Zoo, and though Dad took me and Peter many times later (there are a number of photos of that time), the magic of it all was topped by another experience. Mum and Dad decided to have tea and scones at the tearoom, and we sat on the verandah as the weather was nice. Mum was just saying that a penny was too much for the pat of butter, even if it did have a lion's head on it, when Dad looked up the road and said, 'Frank – look!' and I saw a keeper coming along holding a little crippled boy by the hand. I got off my chair and Dad said, 'Go on'. I got down the steps alone and started hobbling towards them. The keeper stopped and waited, and when I reached them I saw it was a 'monkey', a bit smaller than me. It reached up and took my hand, and we walked down together. When we reached Mum and Dad, Dad thanked the keeper and said, 'That was the furthest he has walked alone,' and the keeper and my friend walked on. I still remember the feel of that strong, bony hand so confidently in mine, as we helped one another. I can't remember if he was ginger or not, but I think so. I don't really know whether they had a young orang-utan at the zoo at that time.

Though I was not aware of it, the family fortunes improved, with Dad neither drinking nor smoking, and Mum's astute shopping, they had a little surplus cash. I understood later that Mum had worked as a cook for a very wealthy and prominent Jewish family, and had become fluent in Yiddish, which subsequently she used to good effect in Jewish bargain stores where she was accepted as one of the tribe and automatically got a reduced price. It meant that when there was an opportunity to buy bankrupt stock, they had the 'readies' to buy whatever (clothes, boots, bed linen, and all sorts of other things) and then sell them on at a small profit, to people who could not afford it in the shops.

Chapter 3   times at Taw Green Mill

Once more I left home. It was the summer of 1931 and I was taken to Devon by my mother's cousins, Ann and Bet, who lived at Taw Green Mill, near South Tawton. I was not aware of the relationship at the time, life was still confusing, and all I knew was that I had lost my family again. But I was soon fascinated by the animals and the poultry. Granny Taylor, Ann and Bet's mother, looked after me and took me out to feed the chickens and turkeys, and picking fruit, and there – without realising it – a love of country and animals was born.

After a while Mum appeared with Peter, and then, after another week or so, Dad arrived for a few days, and we all went home. There are photos of this period. Among many wonderful memories of those holidays, which were yearly, one in particular stands out vividly, and started a life interest in guns, and occurred in 1932.

One morning, while Granny Taylor was giving me breakfast, she said that the squire and his gamekeepers were to try to kill a wild cat that was killing livestock. They thought it was in a strip of conifers that ran from South Tawton to Wood Cottages.
We walked up to Wood Cottages, and followed the men who were spread out across the wood and slowly walked forward watching up in the tree tops, and another line of men was coming the other way. Well, we met in the middle where there was a big thorn bush and brambles, and, as we were standing

around, one man faced the bushes to relieve himself, and fell back screaming – the cat that had been hiding there sprang out and was clawing him, and several men tried to knock it off with their guns, but it broke loose and dashed down the hill through the woods, and the guns were firing, and it went end-over-end and stopped. A man went to it, and fired once more, and then dragged it by its tail up to the squire. It was as big as a dog. I was thrilled by it all and I asked Gran if we could go again.

Another year Granny Taylor took me to watch the squire's men doing the badger management. She explained this kept the badgers healthy and their numbers regulated so they didn't become a nuisance. At the sett they stopped up the exits, dug down to a badger then, using a large calliper like thing, they lifted one badger at a time. I was told they knew where to dig by listening with long rods with ear-trumpets on, and that they had a pair of specially trained terriers who would be put in the sett and who would isolate a badger between them and bark so the listening keeper knew where to tell the men to dig so they came down right above the badger. Once the badger was lifted, the gamekeeper said what it was, male, female, young, old, healthy, diseased or ailing in some other way. At a nod from the squire, the old, ailing and diseased were killed instantly; afterwards the rest were let back into the sett and all went on their way. Back then the landowner's gamekeeper knew his badgers, would have known how many and what to expect from having watched the sett previously, and knew it was important to keep them in balance with the rest of the wildlife.

Over the next few years, until I was 10, we carried on visiting Taw Green Mill in the summer. Once when I was there, Granny Taylor and family were having a pig killed and were very busy. Gran's husband said he wanted me to do an important job, he took me into a loose box and there was a cow. He told me to sit on the bale and watch her and call them when she lay down, for she was going to have a calf. I watched and I could hear the pig squealing and thought I would sooner be there, but I had an important job to do. The pig went quiet and suddenly the cow laid down and started to grunt, so I went to find them, and he said, 'Good boy, just right – look there' and two legs were coming out, then a nose and a head, and – whoosh - the whole calf was there, all wet and steaming. The cow stood and licked it and nudged it and, after two attempts, it stood up! I was amazed, and went up close, and the cow gave a soft 'moo' and gently pushed me away. Mr T said, 'That was a good job done!' so I went and watched them cutting the pig up.

Over those years I grew more confident – I saw foxes, badgers, and helped to catch rabbits and moles, and went round the rat traps and told Granny Taylor when one was caught, so she could deal with it. Once when I told her there was one in the trap, instead of putting the trap in the mill stream to drown it, she opened the trap and let it go, and said it was only 'an old water ratty', and 'would do no harm'. When I read 'Wind in the Willows' years later I knew him!

One year when I was there, she said that we were going to see the Scotsmen bringing the black cattle to Belstone-in-the-Moor to go out on the moor, and we saw them coming up the road. It seemed like hundreds! And the men looked wilder than the cattle! It looked as though their feet and legs were wrapped in sacking, with big bare knees, hairy and raw-looking, and bodies wrapped in old brown blankets, and big brown flat hats on top of masses of hair, and big beards. Granny Taylor said they did not talk English.

They all went out on the moor, and the men stopped, and the cattle went a bit further and stopped, looked around and started to lie down. I thought they were calving, but Granny Taylor said that they were wild cattle, and that, by the time they reached the Scottish border, they had been made docile by not being allowed to lie down to rest, and at least half the men were awake at night keeping them on their feet – fields had been rented at the right distance apart for each day's march for them to graze and drink. The men sat down, and we went closer, and we could not understand them as they talked and ate rubbery grey stocks of porridge, or so I was told. They had walked the cattle all the way from Scotland. I have no dates for those times, but I must have been between 6 and 7 years old – so around 1933.

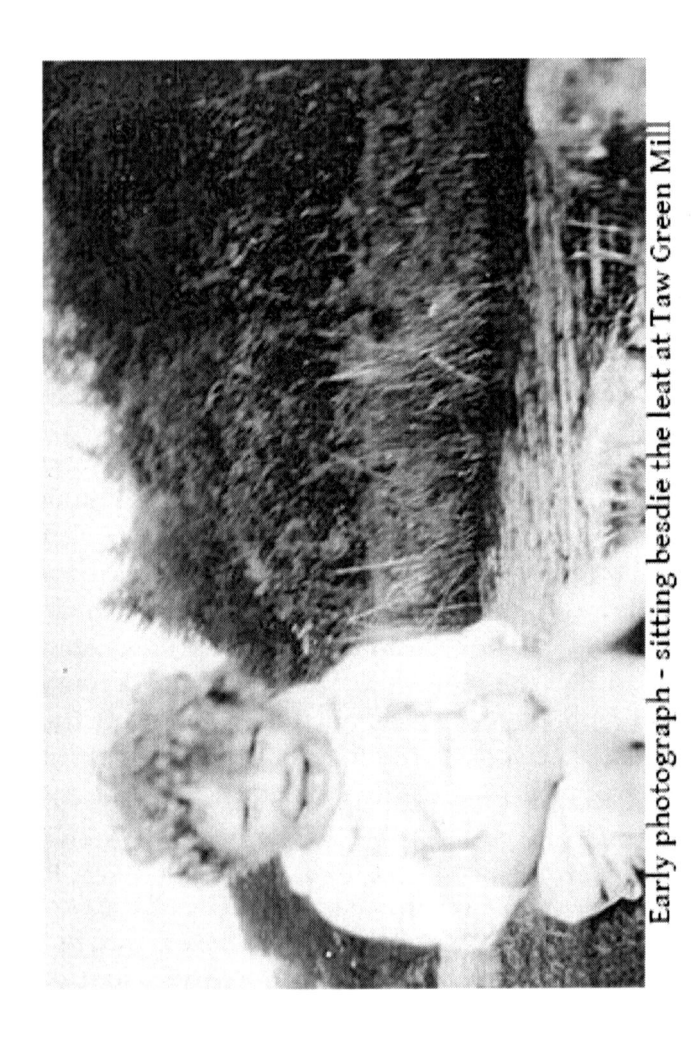

Early photograph - sitting besdie the leat at Taw Green Mill

Feeding chickens with Dad (and unknown boy) at Taw Green Mill

Sitting on the leat wall at Taw Green Mill

Mum, Dad and me at the seaside

Chapter 4   cripple school

I wasn't able to go to school at the normal age because I wasn't steady enough on my feet, so Mum started to teach me how to read, write and do sums. She had been to 'penny-school' when she was young and could read well, write and was excellent at arithmetic. I soon loved to read and write.

However, when I was nearly seven, a new experience started for me – I went to school! It was what was known as a 'cripple-school', where they concentrated not only on the 'Three R's' but also a lot of art work – drawing, painting, modelling, making things out of card. It seemed to me to be more shades of 'He won't be a lot of good then, will he?'

I also soon learned of 'the viciousness of cripples' – I was there to be looked after, but my parents told me that I came home nearly every day with a different bandage on. For example, there was a girl who was like this in a wheelchair, very fat, smelling dreadful and her head seemed to be held on by a big pink thing. She would wait, peeping round the corner of a passage, and when another child came along she would emerge, bowling along fast. You could not escape, and then, emitting a horrible screech, she would slam into you against the wall and then go off gurgling.

At the morning break we got a small bottle of milk and an orange. I soon learnt to put my orange in a pocket and quickly drink the milk and keep moving while I ate the orange, and to stay away from the walls, otherwise the wheelchair-bound would trap you against the wall and take whatever you had. I remember once the oranges were small and bitter, and, as we could not eat them, they were thrown about. I still had mine when the Headmaster came round the classes telling us off. I showed mine, and so did several others. It seemed that the supplier had been left with a lot of Seville oranges for making marmalade, and had unloaded them on us.

We also had midday meals – this was not a usual practice in those days – some of the older boys told me to go and ask 'What's for afters?' at the teachers' tables up on the stage. So I went and pulled on someone's trouser leg and asked, and was told 'Wait and see!' and I returned and said, 'Wait and see' but by then someone had eaten my dinner.

When the ladies came round with the afters, if you hadn't eaten all your dinner they did not serve you your sweet, so whoever had my dinner plate had my sweet as well. This made such an impression on me at this age that I spent the next fifteen years (including the time I was in the Army) holding onto my plate with one hand, ready to stab with my fork any hand that came near, and would react violently against anyone stealing food, especially mine. The 'Wait and See' that lost me my dinner there turned out to be stewed apples and custard and ever after that is what I called that pudding.

For a time, (for a reason that I never knew - perhaps Mum was ill) I had to stay with Granny Buck, and the ambulance for school used to pick me up from there.

I don't know where the school was, as we – that is me and others - were collected from our homes by a big brown and cream ambulance, which was lined with what we call match-boarding, with round wooden buttons covering the fixings.

In the evenings I spent a lot of time with my Great Uncle Dingle, Gran's brother, who lived in the back room. He talked to me about the Great War, where he had been in all the major battles and had the medals. He played First World War songs on his gramophone, which had a big horn on top, to a point where I knew them. Great Uncle George Dingle and I used to sing along with the records, and some of them I still catch myself singing when a bit stressed, usually when a job's not going well, and work mates have asked whether I had a problem as I was singing war songs, and had not been aware that I was doing it. He also told me about the time when the water bowser arrived with the driver - headless - still holding the reins, and how, going on a trench raid, they sharpened their trench shovels because it was a better weapon in close-quarter fighting in the trenches, and how the Germans had to thoroughly clean their gas masks after a gas alert, so our lot would open a couple of cylinders when the wind was right, listen for their gas alert, and when they heard the 'All Clear', wait five minutes, and let the rest go, killing hundreds. He always finished by saying 'The only good Jerry was a dead one, and they will come again, Frankie, and you will be in it!'

It seems funny now that I remember so clearly small instances from this school; for example: two teachers with an umbrella trying to see if a drawing

I made of a man using an axe to cut a tree down was correct, as the axe head, when at the top of the back swing and looking from behind, appeared to be pointing *at* his head and, having swung the 'brolly' around, and having got another teacher to decide that I had it right, then came the question 'How did you know?' I just said, 'I have seen a lot of trees axed'. They did not seem to understand, and they did not understand my compositions about country life: calving, pig-killing and wild-cat shooting either.

Chapter 5   at Woolmore Street School

I don't think I was at the cripple-school long, just a few of terms. When I was about eight, it was decided I was ready for the rough and tumble of Woolmore Street School – and when I was told I was going there I thought so too. However, because some educational bright spark thought I should be introduced to it gently, Mum was told to take me to the Infants' Department at Woolmore Street School – at nearly eight! The Infants' Head Teacher had me read, write and do a few sums, and was surprised how advanced I was. I now think that she was expecting a mental age of about 5. I know the five-year-olds thought so! They began calling me 'silly boy lemon'. There was an older girl there of about seven – I don't know what her problem was but she used to sing nursery rhymes all the time. I think her mental age was low, but she used to taunt me with 'Seesaw, Marjorie Daw, Johnny shall have a new master. He will get but a penny a day, because he can't work any faster', and used to call me Johnny, unwittingly reinforcing those hurtful words 'Won't ever be a lot of good, will he?'

Then I was sent to the Elementary part of Woolmore Street School, and the lady teacher was called Miss Curt. Now, because a number of the boys had sisters or brothers in the Infants they already knew my name was 'Johnny' and I was 'not very with it'. You moved up through the school by your results in an internal exam, I found there were some boys bigger and older than myself who were stuck in class one, possibly because they were slightly deaf or could not see the blackboard too well or were even dyslexic, and undiagnosed in those days. They were invariably put at the back of the class, and would only be moved up in desperation so that room could be made in the first class.

Now things got really tough – I was immediately a target for the bullies, plus my three 'Rs' - reading, writing and arithmetic – were in advance of theirs, which they seemed to regard as my way of 'showing off'. As a result, I was hit most days. As we went home for dinner I was exposed to it twice a day. Quite a few of the boys had not got a dinner to go home to, which did not help. I soon learnt not to put my hand up in class when the teacher asked a question, I'd act like I did not know the answer.

Once, in a reshuffle of seating, I sat by a lad who would root in his hair with his fingers and put a louse on his reading book and kill it with his thumbnail. Next day Mum arrived and marched into the class and told Miss Curt what was happening. She told Mum that it could not happen. Mum said if Miss Curt didn't look, she would! When Mum and Miss Curt looked, Miss Curt was shocked.

Mum told me that the teachers were responsible for the condition of the books and in those days they were just as afraid of the sack as anyone else. Two days later the 'Nit Nurse' arrived and went through everyone's hair. As it happened I never, ever, got head lice, and learnt many years later, that my curly hair, which was such a source of derision and ridicule, was actually a 'no go' area for European or Asian head lice, and, as I did not meet any Africans,

I was immune. Apparently, all the head lice are the same, but their claws have evolved differently for each racial hair-type.

I was still spending my summers at Taw Green, Devon, but after a while Mum would arrive with Peter, then Dad for a few days, and then back to Poplar. I have photos from these times which I will include.

I moved up a class at school – a Mr Fry was the teacher, a portly man in a brown tweed suit. Now there appeared to be less painting and drawing, and learning tables by rote. Sums were put up on the board, and you did them, handed in and they were marked. That would have been all right, but the teacher called out the names of boys who got the most right, and made the ones with none right stay in class during playtime and do them again. So these boys began to ask me the answers and, under threat, I told them, so now the teacher had more boys with the sums right and he realised what was happening and gave them a one-hander each – that is one stroke of the cane. He asked me if I had given them the answers and, like a fool, I said 'no', so he gave me a one-hander for lying. The safest thing for me to do now was to get mine wrong.

This state of affairs did not last long – Mum found out about the one-hander and asked me why. She had me doing sums at home and then she said that I should now put the correct answers in at school. In trepidation, I did, and my book came back marked correct but the teacher said nothing out loud to the class, and I generally progressed reasonably well, but there was always the thought that, with employment as scarce as it was, my prospects were not good, and I also became worried by what I had seen on my way to school.

Chapter 6   the start of my plan

On my way to school, at the end of Robin Hood Lane, just before it meets East India Dock Road, there was a lock-up rag and bone scrap yard, like a cavern, presided over by an old man and woman and, terrifyingly, by the front was a big notice which said, 'They wasted, now they want' and it depicted a man and his wife, plus two children, going to the Workhouse. I didn't say anything to Mum or Dad, but I started to search everywhere for the bottles, rags, bones, scrap metal, and any of the stuff these people would pay you for.

I found that at Blackwall Stairs, at the other end of Brunswick Street near where my Gran lived, I could get down on the Thames foreshore at low tide, where it seemed that every day fresh bits of brass, copper and iron, were exposed by the tide - all of which was taken to the shop to 'keep me from the Workhouse'. On one disused slipway was an old wooden barge rotting away, and around it I found a lot of big iron nails about 3 cm long and about 8 mm tapering to a point. I could not carry them all at once, so I took as much as I could to Gran's and she asked me what I wanted it for. I told her 'to keep me out of the Workhouse'. I said there was a lot more – she gave me an old shopping bag and warned me about the tides. When I took them to the scrap merchants, he gave me nine pence, and asked where they had come from. I just said, 'You don't want any more then?' He laughed and said, 'As many as you like'. I found a tiny carving of a greyhound's head on the foreshore, carved in bone - I still have it eighty years later. *(Photo at end of chapter)*

On the old wooden barges were cast-iron double bollards, one on each side at the bows and the same on the stern, bolted through the gunnels. I began digging away the rotting wood with one of the nails and over several attempts I was nearly there, but when I next went someone had got it free and it was on the shore. I could not lift it so got a bit of old rope and dragged it in behind my Uncle Jim's shrimp boat, moored up there for the winter, to hide it. I knew the tide would hide the drag marks.

It was over a mile to the scrap merchant, so I did it in easy stages, hiding it at the end of every stint over several evenings. When I finally got it there, he asked me my name and only gave me a shilling as I would not tell him. I resented that greedy man – he could have had the other three, but I never went there again - and by chance found another source of income.

On a subsequent visit to Blackwall Stairs, looking down river, I saw a lot of long white strips and, on a closer look, they were lengths of wood six to eight feet long. I had started gathering them, thinking they would break up easily to make penny bundles of firewood, when a voice said, 'And what do you think you are doing?'. I looked up and there was a man standing on the wharf 12 ft above me. I said, 'I'm clearing up this flotsam' he said, 'Come off it, it fell off the wharf, it's never been in the 'oggin' (East End for river), so I said, 'If you want it, then take it back'. I think he did not want the job of retrieving it as he said, 'You had better keep it now'. I asked what they were and he said, 'Off the old oars'.

I gave some to Gran on my way past. A woman called out 'Where did you get the wood, son?'. I told her 'Off the old oars'. She said, 'Disgusting boy!' and slammed her door.

I went home and got busy and made eleven penny-bundles and knocked out (sold) eight that evening. Next day I told Mum where I'd got the wood and what the woman had called me. She told Dad and he said, 'I know that wharf – they make barge oars'. Mum said, 'But the woman had said I told her - you know – loose women (whores).' I was going to drop the lady in some, but not now!

A couple of days later I went straight on to the wharf, and I saw the big band saws cutting out the oar shapes, which were 15 feet long (about 5 metres), and men using big draw knives taking off the edges and producing my long strips. Finally, a man said, 'What are you doing here?' I told him, 'I have come to clear some of those strips away.' He said, 'I don't know anything about that', so I said, 'I have had some before'. He looked at me for some time then said, 'Well you'd better have some more then!'. I thanked him, and staggered home with such a load I was glad to drop some more at Gran's. She had enough, but she sent me to three more houses, where they bought them from me. I already know how many bundles I could have made, so I asked for what I would have made on them, and they paid with a bit extra, so I thought that was 'a bit of alright' as I hadn't had to make the bundles either.

I had learnt something else – if you stand quiet when challenged, and were polite, they were either too busy or too lazy to check up and would either say 'Well, carry on ' or then added 'but don't make a lot out of it.'

Conditions were improving generally. A few more people were finding work, mainly casual, which meant getting up early and doing the rounds of all the likely places to get taken on, and of course for a pittance – perhaps 3 or 4 members of a family leaving early with not much more than a cup of hot water for breakfast, in hopes that at least one of them will arrive home in the evening with a shilling or half-crown so their Mum could pop out and get something for tea. For a lot of East End families the staple diet was bread and dripping (the fat usually from beef and sold off by the butchers and used as a spread and was much cheaper than butter which was a very rare treat.) For many families coal was too expensive so they never had a fire in their cooking range, so they bought in cooked food such as pie and mash, or saveloy and pease pudding, or meat balls and bubble and squeak. Even for those men in work very often the total meat protein for the week was 2 ounces of ham along with a pennyworth of pickle in a screw of greaseproof paper when he came home with his wages on Fridays. Obesity was something you never saw, unless it was a publican, or some married women who were chronically diabetic, usually with large families.

Children from many families would run errands for the better-off, and would, with the few coppers earned, go to the grocers shops to buy broken biscuits (all biscuits were packed in large tins and sold by weight, and as a result there were always some broken that the shopkeeper was glad to clear). By chance our new neighbour happened to be forewomen at Huntley and Palmers at Reading, which for them was a long daily commute, and their old father was supposed to clean and cook for them for when they came home. When Mum got to know them they told her how awful the food he made was, she offered to get their evening meal, and one night they gave Mum a 5 lb bag of broken biscuits explaining that all staff were allowed to buy a bag for a small fee as they left work on Friday when they collected their wages.

Now, a lot of the workers could not afford to buy the biscuits, so Mum arranged that our neighbours should take in some money so that other employees could take up the offer – consequently on Friday nights anything from 15 lb to 25 lb of broken biscuits would arrive, and they could be anything from family assorted to Marmite twiglets. There were cheese flavoured crackers, digestives, plain and chocolate, all sorts of biscuits. Once they were like small boats made of waffles filled with marshmallow and dipped in chocolate. All these goodies were put up in ¼ lb and ½ lb bags, and re-sold to make a small profit for us, and these fed many families, some of whom came to the door every Friday night.

One Thursday night the neighbours told Mum they would not need a dinner on Friday, as their father had promised to do them a chicken dinner. Now on Wednesday evening Dad had found one of his Indian Game hens dead and he told Mum that we couldn't use it, as we didn't know what it died from, so he would wrap it up in newspaper and put it the dustbin - so when the girls said about the chicken dinner he went out in the yard and looked in it and told Mum 'It's ok it's still there'. On Friday morning he put the bin out for collection and checked and said to tell Mum it was still there, so don't worry. Mum said, 'I will do two extras anyway and if it's still not needed it will be all right cold on Saturday'. When Mum had a look in the bin just before the dustmen came, the chicken was gone!

When the girls came home from work, they were in our kitchen in about 10 minutes, and said, 'It was horrible – the chicken had only been roughly plucked, and not even gutted, and he had boiled it in a saucepan, along with peas, which he had not even shelled.'

Later on Dad said we had better be careful what we say in the yard, as the old boy must sit in the outside toilet listening to everything said in other yards. My parents said nothing about the origin of the chicken he'd cooked them and I learned about diplomatic silence.

Things were better at school now. I was not being asked for the answers in arithmetic, and the teacher was handing the book back without comment. Now, when questions were asked, I no longer put my hand up eager to give the answer. If the teacher asked me directly, I would say 'Is it so and so, Sir?' like I wasn't sure and was guessing – that way I avoided antagonising the bullies.

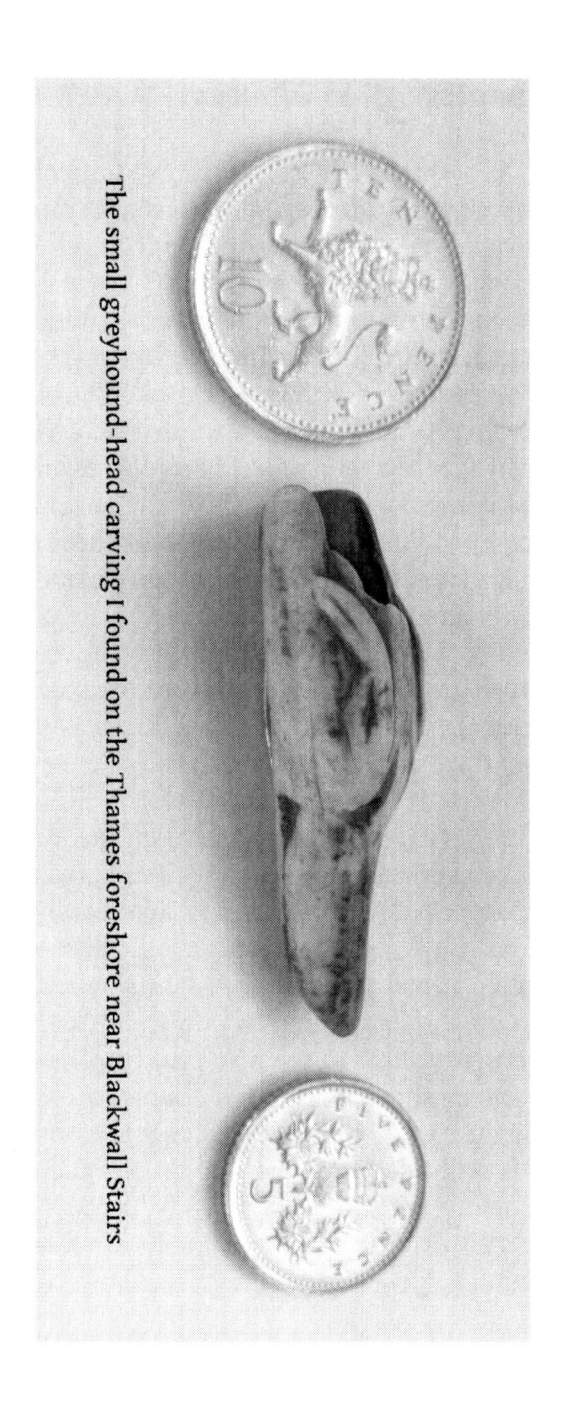

The small greyhound-head carving I found on the Thames foreshore near Blackwall Stairs

Chapter 7   foot notes

In a small lane connecting Woolmore Street to Poplar High Street there was a farriers that was always busy, as between a third and a half of all transport was still horse-drawn. In the wintertime especially I would stay at the door watching, fascinated by the sparks and glowing shoes, and the ring and clang of hammer and anvil. Once one of the farriers came to the door and said, 'Have you not seen shoeing before?' and I said, 'Yes, in Devon, but not in the dark'. I wrote an essay about it once, and got a good mark. The mention of shoes reminds me that a lot of the working class, or 'unemployed' were badly shod, and suffered from corns and bunions. Young women in particular would wear the same shoes until they literally broke up. Most men repaired their family's shoes if they could afford to buy the leather – my Dad did!

There were many cases of people dying of septicaemia through cutting their corns with a razor blade possibly not sterilised adequately. Boot and shoe shops ran 'boot and shoe clubs' - those that could afford the four coppers a week made up a group and, according to how many members there were, drew lots to see who could go and get a pair of boots or shoes, but had of course to keep paying in for the rest. If they thought that their own footwear was still adequate, they could sell their chance to someone in dire need for, say, a couple of weekly donations, and wait for that person's chance to come round again – so when my parents were offered the opportunity to buy a big sack of American baseball boots, they jumped at the chance.

These boots came as part of the ballast in an American ship here to pick up a cargo. A baseball boot, for those who have never heard of them, were of strong canvas with a rubber sole not unlike a trainer, but much thinner. They had a corrugated rubber welt round, and circular rubber shields over the anklebone. The rubber came in red, blue or green, and the boots were unworn. When the sack was delivered Dad and the man had a job getting it down the passage to the scullery. When we looked at them some were in pairs tied by their laces, but most of them were loose and all sizes and all colours.

The next evening Dad tipped them all out, and they covered the floor a foot deep. First of all, we were picking up one of them, then looking for another same size, same colour, until Mum said we were getting nowhere, so Dad had me throwing all blues under the table, all reds under the sink, and greens between the cooker and the corner, and Mum and Dad set about sizing them up. There were some small ones, but most were 6 to 10 s, and there were nearly 300 pairs.

Mum and Dad had already worked out how much they would go for and leave a good profit. The next evening a woman came to the door and asked, 'Have you some of those American boots?' Dad asked what colour and size and said how much, and the lady bought a pair – she was back in 10 minutes with her sister for a pair and was already wearing hers. So, without having to advertise, there they went! There were some left over, like having a size 10 in a blue right, and a green left, so Dad got some odds and ends of paint and made them match, and then they went too!

It seemed that everywhere you looked people were wearing our baseball boots, almost as ubiquitous as trainers today.

Chapter 8   beating the bullies

I was doing better at school now and moving up, but there was still trouble with bullies. It seemed the trouble now was that I didn't rake about at night, nor to belong to any group or because I was going to Sunday School - anything. I was different! So Dad thought I was now strong enough to learn to box, and got a small pair of boxing gloves cheap from a second-hand shop. He had been a heavyweight boxing champion at the Duke of York's Military School for the sons of soldiers who were killed in action, and my Dad's father, who had died of wounds received in the Boer War, was also a heavyweight champion in the Queen's Bays Dragoon Guards - so he knew what to teach me and how.

We began for a short time each evening – Dad believed that most bullies could be stopped with one hard and accurate punch, so time was spent on foot position, distance, accuracy, and delivery of a straight right and with full upper body weight, and only after that did we move on to blocking punches and counter punching. Always this training came with the warning not to look for trouble, but if confronted, don't reply to taunts – concentrate and at the right psychological moment you will find you have struck, and the shock is usually enough to end the confrontation – if not, you have to resume the stance, and a non-antagonistic expression, and concentrate.

In 1935 Poplar borough had built a power station in Poplar High Street and it was now possible to have mains electricity. Gas lights and coal-fired cookers (ovens) were the norm before then. Households that could afford to rent the gas cooker in reality saved by not having to keep a fire in their cooking range in the summer and of course radios were run off accumulators - like primitive acid batteries - that had to be changed by a man in Poplar High Street who had a generator and charging board. I don't know when the electricity cables were laid in the streets at least I can't remember - probably sometime when I was away. Mum and Dad decided to have electricity installed but permission had to be sought from the landlords first, and it was granted as it was an improvement to the property.

The electricity board sent two men who fitted the iron conduit, pulled the wires through, fitted the wooden pattresses held by 3 x 3 inch screws to hold the switches, ceiling roses and bulb holders and the first bulbs all complete to the meter outside the front door, which took a shilling a time, all the lot in one day for no charge. Next day four men arrived, dug up the road and pavement, laid a cable to the meter, restored the road and pavement - and we were modernised and, as with the gas, you could hire or buy a cooker. Dad bought an old mains wireless at some time.

Some time later I came home and there was a blue haze up the street and the tar was melting in a line up the road. Mum lifted me up to pull the switch by the meter down. Dads wireless was wrecked! It seems they had a problem with the generator or too much power had escaped. The board, restored and replaced everything straight away – free - no quibbles.

With the new power supply a man started a bag-wash in the high street – this was a kind of laundry - and Dad saw it as a chance to relieve mum of the Monday drudgery of the weekly wash of sheets and pillow cases. These were now put in a large sack. The man at the shop clipped a label on it and gave you a token. Next day you retrieved your sack - the contents had been boiled, washed and spin-dried and only needed airing and ironing. Of course the small wash was still done at home. Dad made me a barrow to deliver and retrieve the bags as they were quite heavy and I soon had a clientele of people who wanted their washing taken. I charged 6d a round trip and could take three bags at a time and it was not long before I had the business of several boarding houses.

Another thing that was improving people's health was a new scheme of free disinfectant for washing outside lavatories and drains, which was collected from a council depot. You had to take your own bottles and an old man sitting on a box crouched over the siphon in a carboy would fill the bottle and without looking up would keep on muttering 'only one each'. Well by the time I had mine filled, and one for Gran, and one each for three Aunts, and several customers I had quite a few but he went on filling them and I got a couple of pence each for fetching them.

One evening Dad took me to St Georges Hall in East India Dock Road where a young athletic man tried to teach gymnastics with wall bars and a vaulting horse and parallel bars and climbing ropes. I enjoyed that and was soon doing as well as anybody. The only drawback was the vaulting horse. I was in constant fear of putting my hip out again and this was a struggle mentally to launch myself off a springboard and fly over a vaulting horse but I got there and in later life I was very glad I had that experience. I realize now that Dad, without making a big thing of it, was gradually making me as good as anyone else. Maybe his grandmother's words had hurt him too

I carried on earning coppers and Mum put them away for me in my 'workhouse book' as she called it. Dad said once it was good to be thrifty and save but I must keep in mind that when a rainy day came the man who gave his money to the brewer or tobacconist was given an umbrella and that because I had saved I would have to buy my own. It took me a while to work it out. If you had got some money don't tell anybody.

I no longer went to Devon. I think with hindsight Granny Taylor's husband must have died and she had gone to be near her son who was the baker in Ugborough and lived in the end cottage in the same row as the bakery. Instead Dad spent his holiday taking me round the city to the War Museum, The Science and Natural History and art galleries, and of course Regent's Park Zoo and many times to the Tower of London. I never tired of going to the Tower, and there I also began to learn about the early development of firearms, as an example of every development in firearms was there to see.

On my way home with the bag-wash one day two lads stopped me. They wanted to know what I was doing down their street and said it would cost me. I stood between the handles of my barrow. I couldn't do anything. Then one said, 'Or we will tip your barrow over.' I didn't answer, then the other said, 'He must be a dummy.' I hit him – the next thing he was sitting on the pavement holding his bloody nose - I picked up the barrow handles and went on my way.

Though I said nothing to Mum, she sensed something had happed and when Dad came home he asked if everything was all right. I said yes Dad, but later a man came to the door complaining I had broken his son's nose and said I was a vicious little sod and Dad should give me a good hiding. Dad said he would not do that as it must have been provoked and the man said they only asked him what he was going down our street. Dad said you rent houses but you don't own the streets. Good night! I had learnt two things; a straight shot works, and streets were public access. Dad's only comment to me was do not provoke or look for trouble – one other lesson learnt. A victim gets hurt many times, but a good straight shot and the bully cries louder than anybody - and all his followers suddenly lose interest.

The Silver Jubilee of King George the Fifth and Queen Mary 1935 took place and there were street parties for the children and I still have my commemorative beaker, as given to all children by the County Council. *(see photo)*

Up Poplar High Street by the gate to the recreation park were bowling greens. I became fascinated by the accuracy; any attempt by me with a ball produced varying results and often when I was there Dad would go by on his way home. I would fall in beside him and without a word went home. One day a group of boys I did not know stopped and wanted to know what I was watching old men rolling balls around for, but I saw Dad coming and fell in as usual. He asked why I was with those boys. I said I was not. He then said there are two ways you can go in life. You can be a nuisance to society and spend half your life in prison or you can be honest and only possess what you have earned. Choose your friends carefully and he quoted 'birds of a feather'. Even now, I have many acquaintances but few close friends outside of the family.

Chapter 9   new additions

It was now 1936 but, remembering my birth date of the 12th of June, I was still only nine. I was still going to the gym club and one day on the way there Dad asked if I would like to go to a boys' camp in the summer. I agreed. It was being arranged by the youth leader and I had to have a vaccination, which being done, I was supposed to wear a red arm band to indicate that it should not be damaged until the scab had come off. I did not wear the band as it immediately became a target for the bullies! As the year progressed gradually conditions and work increased.

I was still clearing up the wooden boxes at Chrisp Street Saturday market and any odd bins of vegetables or fruit that the stallholders could not be bothered with. Of course it meant I had to remove all the other rubbish to the corporation bins. A big bonus was orange papers. In those days oranges were individually wrapped and to unwrap them the fruiterers used to pour them from the box into a sack and by shuffling the sack from end to end this would remove the papers. They were made of a strong tissue and could be used as nice toilet paper! In those days the majority used newspaper torn up in squares. I usually got enough orange papers to last the family a week.

One day Dad sent me to call the nuns on my own as I was going to have another brother or sister. She was born on the Ides of March and named Dorothy. At this time a few district nurses were appointed.

One came to see Mum and baby and as it was her first maternity case - Dad took a photo for her.

Dad took me to Hendon Air Display and although a couple of passenger flying boats flew over all the rest was about the RAF. One of the demonstrations was bombers attacking a fort and these things came lumbering over so slow it's a wonder they never fell down. As they passed over the fort there were flashed and bangs and smoke poured out and, because my eye level was lower, I saw the man who let it off run out and then the Bristol bulldog fighters came and slowly caught up and guns fired and the crews parachuted down. Later I saw a lorry go out and pick them up and they just threw them in the lorry and the head came off one so they gave it a kick, threw it in and drove off. I thought parachutes couldn't be much good if your head came off - and it worried me quite a while after.

Dad made me a set of wooden airplanes, and even a hanger for them (from a cardboard box), after the visit to the air-show, the poor-quality black and white photograph at the end of this chapter, shows them arranged on what was a piece of (mainly) green carpet – which was my airfield.

The next year, 1937, was momentous in many ways. Dad told Mum he thought there was war coming as the firm he worked for was making battleship grey paint. King George V died and The Prince of Wales abdicated because the government of the day could not see the way clear for him to marry an American divorcee and be crowned King, so his younger brother was crowned instead as George VI, father of the present Queen Elizabeth. There is a photo of me, at a street party in Harrap Street to commemorate the coronation (*I am front left of the picture sitting on a chair*), also a commemorative school photo and a photo of the mug we were given, at the end of this chapter.

Then came an opportunity for the family to improve their prospects. The people that Dad's sister lodged with were moving out and, because Mum and Dad had been long-term tenants of the same landlord, he accepted them as tenants of the vacant house in Blackwall Way (Brunswick Street).

Now this place was going to cost half of Dad's wages because it had five bedrooms plus one small front room by the front door one large front room on the first floor and a basement kitchen and scullery - after living in a two-up two-down it was huge. Dad said if we now worked hard we were 'on the up' because this house was a lodging house for the professionals performing at the Queens Theatre in Poplar High Street not more than 250 yards away.

My paternal grandmum had worked for the Abrahams family, that owned the theatre, and so our family was known to them. Even that may have had some influence on the landlord in my parents' favour.

Dad also impressed on me to work hard at school because you had to have an education to work in any business.

When we took over the house we set to stripping all the old wallpaper and making good the plaster, not only that but we set about making the place bed-bug free and proofed. Bed-bugs were endemic to houses at that time and could travel through the old, crumbly mortar between houses in a terrace, the walls between the houses being only one-brick thick – it was not unknown for someone to drive a nail in a wall to hang a picture – only to knock the brick though into next-door's parlour!

Dad had a sort of light that didn't burn-out in the atmosphere, into which you put a tablet – which then gave off fumes that killed the bed-bugs. We then stopped up any and every crevice and crack in the room, in the plaster, edges of skirting boards, window frames etc, so there was nowhere for them to hide. This was done using a form of papier-mâché.

Dad borrowed a large mincer from work and I fed the paper into it, this was then mixed with a quantity of glue and anti-fouling paint. Dad was lucky in that his firm gave him some cans of this from an over production that were left in the stores. This paint was usually used on the ship's hulls and was poisonous, killing any marine creatures that tried to attach themselves the boat - and bed-bugs too in our case. When all was sealed and bug-free they painted the walls in pastel colours. Mum and Dad bought in cheap furniture in white wood and we rubbed it down and painted to match the rooms.

In a partitioned corner of the scullery was a bath – it was big and was made of thick clay like the old-fashioned butler type sinks. I sometimes now wonder whether it was really a big salting vat. Anyway the water was heated by a gas-fired boiler outside and a pipe through the wall. The boiler was filled by a tap over the top. Luxury - we had never had a bathroom before!

MAY CORONATION 1937

KING GEORGE VI

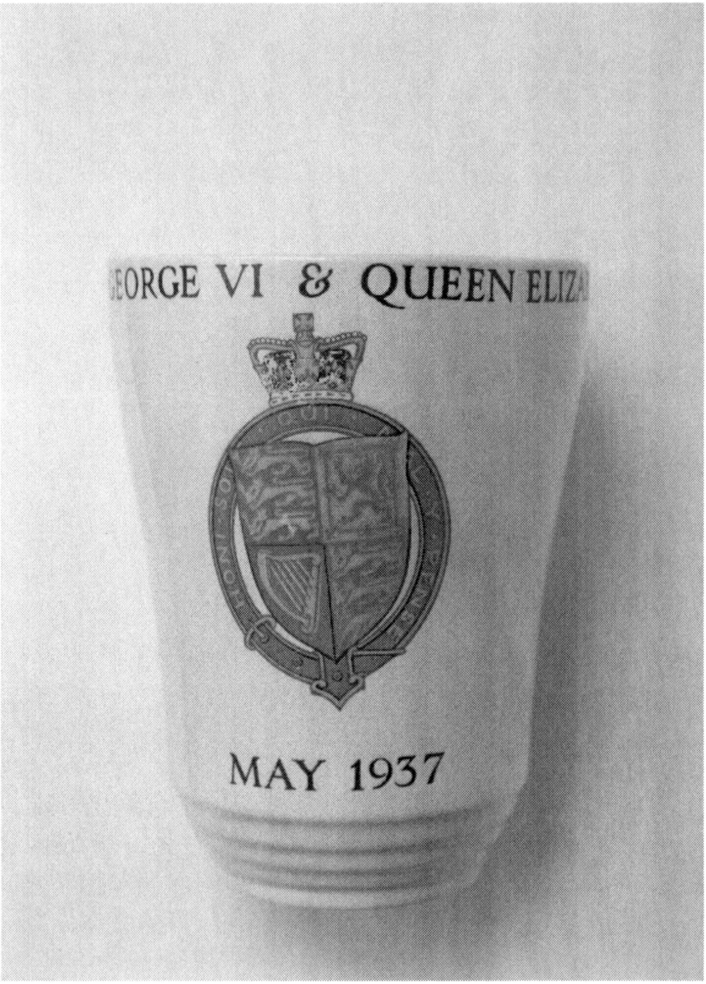
EORGE VI & QUEEN ELIZ
MAY 1937

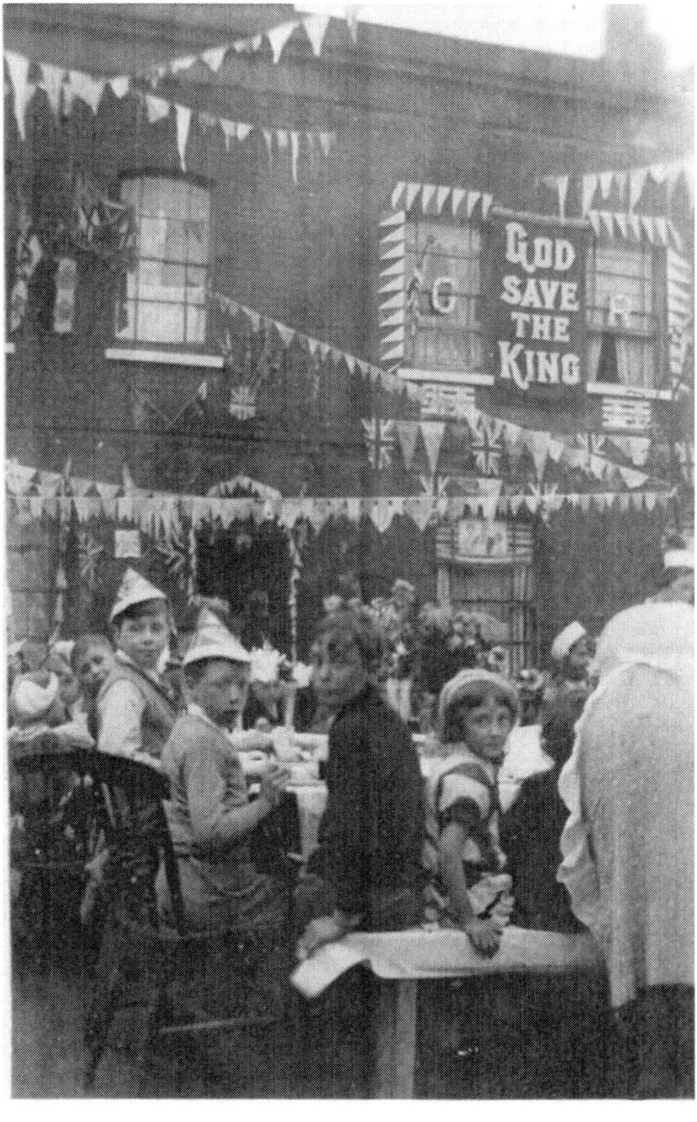
GOD SAVE THE KING
G
R

Look carefully and you can see the planes
Dad made for me, as well as a fuel-pump,
trucks and the 'hangers'.

Chapter 10   boys' camp

Nobody seemed to do anything about birthdays back then but I must have had mine, then it was school holidays and I was off to boys camp.

I cannot exactly place where it was it but turn right out of the camp gate and you went over sand dunes. It was not like Southend; there were no houses, sea food stalls, pubs or ice cream shops and inland it was all fields with wide ditches full of water and small bridges with gates and it was explained to us the gates on the ditches were to stop all the fresh water from draining away and stop the sea water at high tide from coming into spoil the fresh water.

When we first arrived we went into a large hut, which was the dinning hall, and the camp commandant told us the camp rules, one of which was 'nobody was to go in any other tent uninvited'. Then we had a tour of the camp - the latrines, the doctor's tent and surgery and finally our tents, three in a row slightly apart from the rest with a notice saying East End.

They were bell tents with ground sheets and palliasses on the grass floor and three blankets. We gradually took in our surroundings and the other boys at the camp, who all talked posh. I now think we were some sort of experiment. We wandered about the camp awhile and some other boys came back from a day trip. They did not say anything but followed us about talking amongst themselves so we walked out of the camp and onto the beach. We had been told to go to the dining hall at 7 o'clock. We had said we didn't have a single watch among us so we sat on the dunes outside the camp until we saw people heading for the hall.

When I finally got through the door in the dim light someone on my right put a large square piece of fruitcake in my hand with a biggish piece of cheese on the top. I wondered how many I had to share it with. The boy behind was getting the same and a mug of cocoa was put in my left hand when I ate cake and cheese together I discovered a taste to which I have been mildly addicted all my life.

In the camp it seemed strange. I think now that London boys are quick to register distrust or suspicion on the part of others so apart from meals and, of course, the cake and cheese we stayed out of the camp.

On the second day we were leaning over some railings watching some fish in the ditch, which went down to the sea and there was a pair of gates like the lock gates on the docks at home and as we were watching and talking a voice said I hope you boys are not throwing stones in the sluice gates. Being as we disclaimed all responsibility he laughed and said he was fishing on the freshwater side and had to come and see who was about. Over the other side of the road he had a tent and a small boat and he explained how the sluice gates closed as the tide rose and stopped the seawater from spoiling the fresh. He spent his holidays fishing the dykes for roach, and showed us one - the bright silver belly and iridescent red sides beautiful - and I was hooked. I had seen a lot of fish in the aquarium at Regent's Park but this was something different.

Late one night someone heard muttering outside the tent and we all nudged awake and suddenly the sides of the tent swooped in around the middle pole and as we struggled out we heard chuckling but strangely not one of us had made a sound.

The other two tents had collapsed as well so a short council of war was needed. It was decided that it was the toff lot and the best way was for a few of us to sneak round and collapse the camp commandant's tent and sneak back before he came out. This we did – and soon he was shouting and the other staff came out in their dressing gowns. By then we had our lanterns alight and were trying to sort ourselves and our collapsed tents out. It was obvious to us that, as our lanterns were bobbing about, they would come running over thinking that it must have been the East End boys up to mischief, but, when they saw the state we and our tents were in they set to driving in the tent pegs and settling us down.

They asked if we knew who did it. If they had known us better they would realise East Enders never grass, especially to authority - even about enemies. We dispensed our own justice at breakfast next morning.

The camp commandant was still in a temper and said he was disappointed at the behaviour of some campers, who he had thought would have been the better example, to attack his tent and then the tents of our East End guests. We thought that was a bit much calling us 'guests' as we had worked and saved up to come. We would not have had charity. We could see by expressions who was guilty and over the coming week many elbows got nudged when they were carrying their dinner plates.

  Not all the East End lads were known to each other, for example only five of us were from St Georges Hall out of at least 20 as not everybody could afford the vaccination plus the camp fees even though, as we found out later, it had been reduced for us disadvantaged East Enders - a source of resentment among the toff lads. Anyway some of the lads that we did not know personally had haircuts that we used to call topiary-all-of which was clipped off all over except for a tuft at the front. Not only was it cheap it also prevented lice infestation and was generally seen as a poverty indicator. One day one of these lads was ducking down to come out of his tent as another was ducking down to go in. The result was a collision of the upper teeth of one biting into the top of the head of the other resulting in a semi-circle of slots oozing blood so we took him to the doctor's tent. He was not there so we did not go in - as per the rules.

He finally came over and said he had been told the East End boys were round his tent. We showed him the damage and we explained how it happened. He said, 'Thank God for that. I thought I was witnessing the first case of the promised cannibalism.' Whereupon he was informed by us that cannibalism started at Canning Town Bridge as we still had our missionaries, an East End joke, and this army doctor who had spent most of his life in India actually went ahead and asked what form the cannibalism took and was straight facedly told that 'they had babies all year round and shared them out at Christmas.

Any left over were Christmas dinner.' He spluttered a bit and said, 'Good God!' and got on with treating the teeth marks muttering 'Good God' then one of the lads said, 'How much will it be. We've had a whip round.' He said, 'You don't pay me,' 'But we always pay the doctor Sir.' came out reply 'Well you do not here' he said. 'It's free.' and we said thank you and he said, 'As a matter of interest how much did you think I'd charge.' 'Well sir that's what worried us – we only had nine pence halfpenny between us.'

That evening at supper the doctor came upon the stage and recounted the whole incident of the item of the bitten head. We were amazed when he said that we had confirmed in all seriousness that there was cannibalism practiced in the East End but much further East and added he would not explain in public the form that this practice took but would divulge it privately. Then he went on to say that we 'were prepared to pay for the treatment and offered nine pence halfpenny and before those sniggering broke into laughter I will tell you that was the total assets of the whole group and when you consider their circumstances, I consider that they were offering a very high fee. The widow's mite springs to mind. I have heard them described as uncouth. I found them polite and articulate and a pleasure to talk to and thankful and furthermore the lads who came and told me the East Enders were in my tent in mischief had better not come to me with minor scrapes of cuts for I shall not be as Christian as our East End lads.'

Then the Parson got up and said, 'Five of the East Enders came to the chapel on Sunday morning and I did wonder what to expect but they knew the service and responses and, amazingly, the hymns and it was refreshing to hear them singing so confidently unlike some of the strained performances I usually have to endure, and when the congregation left they stayed by the door and when I approached offered me money as they could not see the collection box and furthermore I asked the camp commandant how many East End lads we had. It seemed one fifth had joined my congregation. If one fifth of the campers and staff had come the chapel would have burst at the seams.'

We carried on finding our own interests outside the camp even though the attitude towards us had changed. The evening before we left the camp commandant got up on the stage and said, 'Our East End lads are leaving tomorrow and I have been delighted by their behaviour and good manners and I must say that as to the bad language and vandalism we were told we must expect when these lads arrived; the purveyor of those myths could not have been further from the truth. Some of these lads have asked if they can come again - I have given a whole hearted, yes.' The hall erupted in enthusiastic clapping which left us mystified.

A photograph taken at the boys camp (extreme left)

I still have two of the 'Guest Books' from 7 Blackwall Way – covering the dates from January 1938 to August 1940

Chapter 11 running the pro-house

On returning home I found the family's business was up and running and bookings were coming in from the pros (professional acts) who had stayed there in the past (before we were running it) and those who had already visited expressed delight at the new décor and furniture and Mum's cooking.

Another surprising thing was the tradesmen that called – bakers, grocers and greengrocers bringing samples of their produce because it was an establishment whose food requirements each week was worth courting - even the Co-op delivered a box full of samples. What a change, traders giving us food when ten years previously my parents were in a starving condition as were thousands of others.

Now my life changed again as I now had daily jobs and weekend jobs. If we had Chorus girls in, every evening they needed hot water to wash their leg make-up off, all that had to be carried up two flights of stairs and brought down again. On Sundays the pros left to go to their next venue and the fresh lot would arrive from mid-afternoon to late evening, according to how far they travelled, always by public transport. I only remember one group who had a car.

Dad bought a goblin vacuum cleaner so on Sunday as the guests left my job was to strip the beds and dust the furniture, mantelpiece, windowsills, skirting boards and doors and then change the paper in the drawers. Mum had bought a big roll of the paper from a wholesaler. It was printed with a lavender pattern and smelt faintly of lavender, which seemed to increase when shut in the drawer.

Dad fumigated the rooms, because bed-bugs would also travel in people's luggage (Oddly enough, this has been reported recently as a 'new' problem with people travelling from other parts of the world and bringing bed-bugs home with them!) then vacuumed the house from top to bottom and then we carried up the clean linens and towels for the new arrivals and Mum made the beds.

Some of them had stayed there before with the previous proprietors and, having turned down the beds to see if they were clean, expressed delight at the décor and condition which made us wonder what it was like before. As Mum had been a cook for wealthy people, such as the Liptons tea family, she knew how things should be and, within the general expectation of returns, treated the guests so well that soon the news spread among the pros and bookings came in well in advance.

One act called 'The USA Three' comprising of two men, one with a false leg, and a lady. The booked one double and one single. It appeared that the one legged man and the lady were married and naturally used the double, but she kept face powder and lipstick and other make-up articles on the mantelpiece in the single so that should their agent visit they would appear as three single persons. Married persons in the profession were paid less than two singles!

When bookings were made the guests usually asked for a hot meal. On arrival one group said they always had a cheese and potato pie and stipulated quantities of each ingredient. Mums said to Dad 'This is ridiculous – there are only three of them and this amount would be a big meal for double that number.'

Dad said, 'Do what they ask – perhaps they want the rest cold for lunch on Monday.' When they arrived Mum took them up and said she would bring up their pie. When she placed it on the table they stared at it and said, 'We're afraid there has been a terrible mistake.' Mum said, 'I don't think so – I used the quantities you asked for.' They said, 'But we never get anything like that amount and we did ask a landlady some time ago for the recipe and that was the quantity she said she used. Could you use what we don't need?' Mum said, 'You take what you need – I won't bill you for the rest.' When she came down Mum told Dad she thought landladies had been feeding their own families by cheating the guests.

One guest, who was a magician, on being presented with his bill, pointed out that Mum had forgotten the cruet. Mum never charged for a bit of salt and pepper – apparently landladies would charge as much as half a crown 2/6d for the use of the cruet. He said that at one place they charged that much. It was quite a nice silver plated stand with lead crystal salt, pepper and vinegar containers so he packed it and while he was waiting for his train at the station he heard a shout of 'There he is!' and the landlady came running down the platform followed ponderously by a police sergeant who said, 'This lady accuses you of stealing her family heirloom cruet.' The ex-guest said, 'I have got it - but I bought it,' and showed the sergeant the bill which had as an item – 'cruet 2/6d'. 'Well that's plain enough Sir – you have the receipt though I do think you have taken advantage of a mistake on the part of the good lady.' So the departing guest said, 'As it is a family heirloom I will sell it back for 5/- (five shillings) so make up your mind. My train is coming in.' She paid up. Was that justice? – I don't really know but when you think of all the paperwork and court appearances and solicitors and cost to solve that problem today, I wonder.

Chorus girls had an agent who got their bookings, arranged their train tickets, found and booked the lodgings, arranged the menu and portions, collected their pay as a group, paid all the expenses, deducted his own wages and expenses, but never stayed in the same lodgings. The girls cash wages could be as little as 10 shillings, as they improved and found bookings at better venues their take-home pay improved. Before I ever saw them in the flesh, literally that is, I was often taken to the Queens Theatre and the chorus was on stage. From the upper circle they looked tiny and because all their legs and arms moved together I used to stare hard to try and see the wires that jerked them up and down. I could not imagine several human beings able to move like one.

As for in the flesh, when our first lot returned from the theatre one evening Mum asked me to carry up the hot water to wash their leg make-up off so up I went, knocked on the door and one called, 'If it's a man, stay out, if it's a woman come in'. What a way to confuse an 11 year-old *boy*, so in I went. I was amazed at the sight of ladies with nothing on and suddenly they realised and disappeared behind towels, furniture and odd items of clothes. I put the bucket down and went down the stairs faster than I had ever done! When I went in the kitchen Mum said you didn't spill any water on the stairs did you, only wet lying on the stairs can be dangerous. Mum took their supper up and brought down the dirty water. When Dad came in Mum said, 'Someone won't need taking to the National Gallery.' It puzzled me for a long time that did, until sometime later a lad at school said his father had taken him to the National Gallery to see all the naked ladies painted by the old masters hundreds of years ago. The fathers did this to save their sons from trouble over sexual curiosity.

Because Mum and Dad now had ready cash they were offered all sorts of opportunities such as bankrupt stock, insurance loss adjusters sell-off, offers from salvage agents. If my parents thought whatever was offered could be sold on, subject to its provenance, they would buy a minimum lot. I was very adept at finding customers and there were still a lot of unemployed and very low-paid that were glad of cheap clothing and, in some cases, food. Because of the work I was putting in Mum and Dad bought me a barrel of black treacle as salvage from a floundered ship – it must have been about ten gallons. I had to go to ship chandlers and buy a syrup tap, like a knife blade, that cut off the flow – it cost me 1/6 (one shilling and sixpence). Dad made me a trestle to put the barrel on and now I had to collect 1 and 2 pound jam jars which were costing me 1 and 2 pence each as that was cash back on their return. So having got a dozen together I started filling them after school after my other jobs. Mum put the word about and customers started coming to buy at four pence a pound, a penny back on the jar or seven pence for two pounds plus two pence on the jar and they were soon bringing their own jars which I filled for the straight three pence or sixpence according to size - and the money rolled in to my workhouse book. When the barrel was empty I had made £2 2s 3d (two pounds two shillings and three pence) equal to a man's wage and the customers asked if I would get more - but most of these chances were one-offs – however, many hard-up families had lived on bread and black treacle for weeks.

Mum and Dad did make a mistake once – they bought in half a dozen bottles of port, bankrupt stock, saw the documents, seemed OK, the price was average for this commodity. Great Aunt Blanch bought two which they let her have at cost. Her husband was a small builder and they considered themselves a cut above us but were very paternalistic towards us. Anyway her husband had a glass or possibly two and was ill and their son who was a policeman came and saw Mum and Dad and did an experiment. They opened another bottle, poured some into an enamel plate and set light to it. When the flames died down and went out, what remained was a lilac coloured wax - so even then there were counterfeit products. They poured the rest down the drain. Dad said to Mum, 'I thought only pigs came in pokes.'

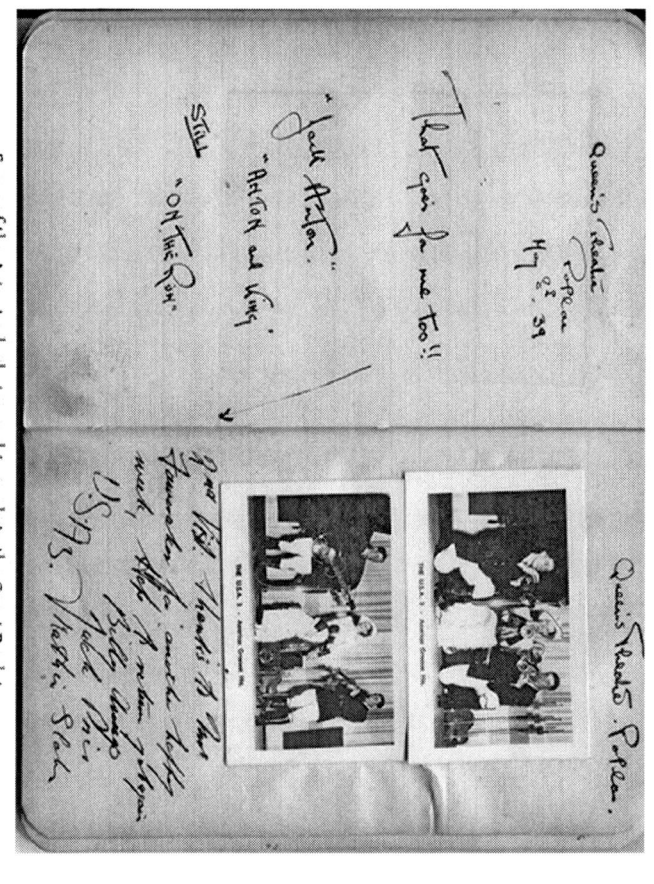

Some of the Acts stuck photographic cards in the Guest Book too – as here from the USA 3 – or, over the page, 'La Desiree'.

Jesse & Pearl
Sept 1939

With very many
thanks to Will
Foreacher for his
care & attention,
hope to see him
yet by gone
Pardon.

La Desiree

Chapter 12   of mice and teachers

On Saturdays Chrisp Street market stayed open for as long as people were buying, and Bretts' had a cake stall which they set up outside the shop. At about five o'clock the girls made tea in a room upstairs and, two at a time, we went upstairs for a slice of bread and jam and a cup of tea – meant to keep us going until, perhaps, eight o'clock. As soon as the market went quiet Brett would say 'pack up' and as soon as the stall was back inside the shop I was finished. The veg and fruit traders would have left and I joined Jack Fairhead who had already started clearing the stalls. Our reward for tidying up the stall areas like this was the wooden crates, plus any odds and ends of fruit and veg – which we always shared. We then carried all the crates to my home, as I had more space in the back yard to put them.

On Sunday Jack would come round and we would make up our penny-bundles of firewood from the crates. On one particular morning Jack arrived as usual and we started splitting the boxes, chopping to length and tying up our penny-bundles when my mother came to say 'There's a mouse behind a wardrobe in a lady's room,' and for me to catch it. So I picked up a piece of sacking and we followed Mum upstairs. She knocked on the door and went in – and soon she called us in. I knew this lady was one of the fan-dancers.

I lifted one side of the wardrobe away from the skirting and the mouse ran to the other side. I said to Jack, 'If you wriggle your fingers on the other side Jack, I'll catch it.' I heard mum say something but, though not wanting to take my eyes off the mouse,

I gave a quick glance up. I saw Jack's eyes were locked solid on the lady, who was taking breakfast, sitting sideways to the table, one long leg crossed over the other with her slipper, a mule type, balancing on her toes. Mum said, 'Move Jack,' and he came out of his trance and did as I asked. As I felt the mouse hit the sack I screwed it up to carry it off downstairs as Jack followed – he literally came out of the room backwards. I heard mum say, 'You better turn round to go down the stairs Jack.'

When we returned to the yard I had to urge Jack to get on with the job as I had to get finished so I could deliver Gran's firewood before lunch. Finally we finished and divided them between us and home he went without a word and I thought no more about it.

When I went to school on Monday, there were other boys still arriving, but before I reached the classroom I could hear a a noise going on and Mr Carter, the teacher, shouting 'What's the reason for this disturbance?' They all went quiet as he picked up his cane and gave his desk an almighty whack and said. 'I asked a question, and believe me; I am going to get an answer. Be sure every-one of you will feel my cane.' He added whacking a pile of books on his desk, his face looked like he was really mad.

Some brave soul piped up 'Foweraker has naked ladies in his house, Fairhead said so, he's seen them.' At that moment I regretted being so close to the teacher as he roared, 'Naked Ladies?' I said, 'She was not naked, sir, she had cami-knickers and a negligee on.' And he instantly gave me a whack across my legs, saying, 'And what was this woman doing?'

'Having breakfast, sir,' which got me another whack, followed by the next question, 'And what were you doing in this naked woman's room?' 'Catching a mouse behind her wardrobe, sir, and my mother was there,' which only earned me another whack and yet another question, 'What kind of establishment do you live in boy?' I answered using the vernacular, 'In a Pro-house, sir...' about to go onto explain that meant it was for professional stage people only – but he's reacted to the words 'pro-house' and whacked out several more cuts on my legs and told me to go and sit down as he didn't want to hear another word from me. I sat down and seethed, trying to work out how to get my revenge. On a teacher? Impossible.

I carried on climbing toward the top of the class in exams, and we now had extra time at school in carpentry classes, which were held in a separate building. I still have a stool I made there. Then, one morning, out of the blue, Mr Carter said to me, 'Do you know The Steamship?' naming the public house at the top of Harrap street. I realised he already knew the answer so could not deny it, then to my amazement he said, 'You can bring me my dinner from there at lunch-time.' He just took it for granted I would do it – had he forgotten already? So when the bell went and we were dismissed I went off, past my home, and on to The Steamship and said what I had come for. Dolly Money, the pub landlord's daughter, looked surprised by said nothing, and gave me the tray of meat and two veg, plus a pudding and custard covered with a tea-towel.

Off I went, as I was passing my home, Mum came out on the balcony and called out to say my dinner was ready. I shouted back that I wouldn't be long and turned the corner into Robin Hood Lane. After about ten paces I threw the lot over the Blackwall tunnel entrance wall to crash down the stairs, say ten metres below, turned round and went home.

Mum gave me a look but said nothing. I had my dinner, did a few small jobs and set off back to school. As I went through the gate Mr Carter shouted at me 'Where's my dinner? You should have brought it straight back. You've eaten it!' I said, 'Two big boys tried to take it off me, and I threw it over the tunnel wall to stop them stealing it.' 'You're lying!' he roared. I said, 'I'm not – I'll show you,' and bolted back down Robin Hood Lane.

By the time he caught up with me I was laying on the top of the wall and he was already not looking too bright. I said, 'Scramble up, sir, you can see it.' By the time he managed to get his stomach on the top of the wall, which was about six foot up, but with a little squint (sloping ledge) half-way up that you could use to push yourself up from, his face was a funny colour. I said, 'wriggle forward a bit more and you'll see it.' He did and gave a groan as he looked down the thirty-odd foot drop to where his dinner lay - I think he wasn't good with heights. We got down and I said, 'Shouldn't we be in school by now, sir?' and dashed off.

I really don't know how far behind me he was, but I arrived just before Mr Wenzel, the head-teacher, came in with another teacher. He looked at the register, and said, 'Call the roll here, then the lesson should be maths, get them started.' As he went out of the door we heard him say 'There you are! My office, I will have an explanation.'

It was sometime before Carter returned to our class and he seemed very quiet and remained like that for the rest of the day. When he dismissed the class he actually said, '... and when leaving go quietly – please.'

Chapter 13   the church and decisions

I was going to senior Sunday school and Church in the morning, after my house cleaning, and in 1937 I received a prize book from All Saints Poplar for my knowledge of the scriptures.

I went on a Sunday school outing and as we were getting in the coach I was given a marzipan fish wrapped in cellophane and an orange. I then realised why the attendance of Sunday School went up before Easter and back to three or four after. When we arrived at the destination we went in to a hall. Tables were laid out with sandwiches and cakes, well, the rapidity with which they disappeared - a plague of locusts could not have done better.

I did not join in the games but wandered off. I found an old horse on a rough bit of land and talked to him for a while. When I went back to the gate he followed me. When I got home Mum said, 'Make any friends today?' I said, 'Yes.' I now believe they were a bit worried by my loner attitude.

During one of the build-ups of attendance at Sunday school, three children came from one family. After about twice, when the time came the teacher handed round a collection box made of papier-mâché in the shape of a lantern and each of the sides showed a picture of a little African boy with a swollen stomach and legs and arms like sticks. Well they always got my penny after the collection. The three brothers started crying and when they were asked what was wrong one said he had a penny and a half crown and had accidentally put the half crown in and he had to buy some shrimps for the family tea. Well the teacher was stumped for he could not break open the box to find out and as a Christian could not disbelieve them so reluctantly, I thought, gave them half a crown which he possibly could ill afford and made them put their penny in the lantern. I think he was conned, but as a Christian I could not say it so as the commandment said 'thou shalt not bear false witness'.

I started confirmation classes and became a star pupil receiving a second prize book from All Saints Church Poplar 1938. I still have both books. I also joined the scouts attached to the church and became reasonably proficient in semaphore, but when the leader started to push me to buy a uniform I dropped out. I could not see the point in having to buy special clothes for a few hours a week.

One Sunday morning I arrived at the church to find no-one waiting to go in so thinking I was late I pushed open the inner door. The church was empty – maybe I was too early - so I crossed the road so I could see the clock. No I was late, but not that late, so I pushed the door open again and the vicar was standing by the altar in his vestments and when he saw me he flipped his hand at me to go and went into the vestry and came out unvested to me and said go home and tried to give me a Sunday school attendance stamp. I would not take it as I had not been to Sunday school and went home.

Later I heard the congregation had warned the vicar they would not tolerate his high church attitude and, as he persisted, had voted with their feet and as they were the wives of local business men and dignitaries he was sacked and a new one installed. It shook my faith that a servant of God could be driven out by the well-off. Or was it the loss of their donations?

Soon after the new vicar arrived he started to arrange a confirmation service. I had been thinking long and hard about what it actually would mean and what the Ten Commandments literally meant. I felt could not aspire to anything that perfect and furthermore, if Great Uncle George was right, I would be forced to break one in time - so I declined.

Sometime later I arrived home and there was an elderly gentleman sitting in the kitchen and he asked Dad if I was the young man in question. Apparently he was Father something-or-other (I have forgotten his name) – he wanted to question my decision not to be confirmed. 'I want you to change your mind and to say what your objections are.' (Only so he could counter them) He said how magnificently I had done in the classes and reminded me about the books, so I said, 'Excuse me' and got up, 'But I am not quite finished yet,' he said. I said, 'I'll fetch the books for you,' He said, 'No, I have not come for the books,' and turned to Mum and Dad and asked if they had any influence. Dad said, 'I did not influence Frank to attend church or Sunday school, that decision was Frank's and so is this.' The Father left - and life went on.

Chapter 14 back to boys' camp

Dad was doing night classes in first aid, so he could look after his own, he said, and there was bad news coming out of Germany. On the newsreel we saw the Nuremberg rally and thousands of Germans roaring Sieg Heil and a little fat boy bashing a drum and I have never forgotten him for as I watched a shudder went through me. I saw him as the one great uncle George Dingle warned me about. We also saw the Nazis burning great piles of the Jews books. I know it is ridiculous but I find it hard to destroy books even now, even obsolete instruction manuals.

Jewish children were brought to England, and some of our theatrical guests, returning from bookings in Germany, confirmed the poor state of the populace if you were not a Nazi party member, life was hard.

I continued physical training at St George's Hall and in due course revisited the boys camp again. This time our tents were with everyone else. There were just a few of us from before. I had got myself a fishing rod and reel from Wells' junk shop in Poplar High Street. Two or three of the others had rods so we were off fishing most days and, without us asking, the cook made up sandwiches for us as we were not appearing for lunch. One morning three of us set off to walk to a green headland we could see from the camp, with the sea to our left and the fields separated by wide ditches to the right.

After a while we saw a field of sheep, one of which had fallen into the water and could not get out and had been there for some time for it was so saturated only its head and neck were exposed, so we went over and caught hold of it. I said, 'You have to grip the wool each side of the jaw.' but we were not tall or strong enough to pull it up so we held on until we saw a car coming up the road. Two men got out and ran over and shouted 'What are you boys doing?' but realising the situation they took hold and had great difficulty pulling it out. Once out it just stood there with the water pouring out of its wool. He asked how long we had been holding it up. Well we did not know because we had no watch, but he gave us one shilling and sixpence anyway - and we went on our way.

Soon after we saw a castle a bit inland and headed for that across the field. We seem to have left the ditches behind, we went through some woods and we wandered around discussing the state of it and came across a large stone cannon ball and sat near it and had our sandwiches. A man approached - he was obviously a gent, he had a tweed suit on and beautiful brown shoes - and he asked how we had got there. We said across the fields. Somebody asked was it his castle. He must have been listening to us talking for he said, 'And what is your interest in the cannon ball?' We said it must have been a big gun – have you still got it? His reply was alas no. Then someone said, 'We have a gun that could spit it out. It would take about twenty pounds of powder in corns as big as cherries.' He said, 'Indeed and where do you keep this monster of a gun?' 'In our tower Sir.' I thought he was looking a bit annoyed because he snapped out 'And where is this proverbial tower?' 'It's the Tower of London Sir'. He started to laugh and then guessed we had come from the camp and told us the path to take to the main gate and to hurry back to camp as time was getting on. When we arrived at the camp a shout went up 'There they are' and a bell started clanging away like mad.

They told us then as we hadn't appeared for tea they were getting worried and had been out searching the dunes and salt marshes. The camp commandant told us to get along to the kitchen to see if cook had saved us any tea. We were in luck. At suppertime the camp commandant was on stage and called us three up on the stage and he thought to repay for the concern we had caused. We said we were sorry for that and our intention was to walk to a beautiful green hill we could see in the distance. He broke in to say we would never walk there and back in a day because it's too far. 'Well it looked near enough yesterday, Sir, but it looks further away this morning.' Some of the campers had a giggle and he turned to them and said, 'How many of you can honestly put your hand up and tell me they know the why this is - and I shall probably ask each of you. I see just four out of sixty two and they are experienced camp leaders. And the answer, gentlemen, is that atmospheric conditions alter the perception of distance. Now carry on lads.' So we recounted rescuing the drowning sheep and had been given one and sixpence for our trouble. He asked where the money was now. Well we looked at one another with the same thought – is he going to take it off us. He realised what we were thinking and 'No, no lads – I do not wish to steal it. I only wish to confirm it. We reluctantly showed it. I had the sixpence so he turned to others and said, 'If you want to split the shilling the burser will gladly oblige – now carry on.' 'Well after a while we could not see the hill but saw a castle instead and went there instead. It took a while but finally we got there, looked around it. It was a bit tumbled down - not a patch on the Tower of London so we headed back. Sorry Sir we did not know we were supposed to check out.' And then he confused us by saying that we were not prisoners and were free to come and go at will. And he was pleased to see we had an adventurous spirit.

The next evening after tea he was on stage again and called us on stage again and when we were there turned to the hall and said it would appear that our intrepid friends did not tell us the whole story yesterday. I thought 'what now?' He went on to say the steward of Sir or Lord so and so (I forget which) had phoned to say that his nibs had discovered three trespassers in his castle ruins. The camp commandant then said that he was shocked and had began to apologise, but the steward said that an apology was not necessary and that his Master, subject to confirmation from me, had offered an invitation for the following Tuesday afternoon to visit the castle and gardens and use the swimming pool, if we so wished, from where we would be summoned for tea at three-thirty and he suggested a party of boys, suitably supervised, of fifteen. And needless to say I have accepted.' He then turned to us with a big smile on his face and sternly said, 'Now perhaps you will recount the whole truth.' By the time we finished and answered questions, it was nearly suppertime. If all this seems trivial it must be remembered that the average East End boy scarcely moved out of a square mile in his life and usually met and married within it, unlike modern children who seem to wander the earth.

At the end of that week a lot of lads dressed as sailors arrived - apparently they were Barnardo's orphans that had been accepted into a naval school at what age I do not know. My own father had been accepted into a Military School aged nine. So perhaps these lads were the same. They were older than us by a year or eighteen months. Even though they had been together for years they did not know each others names and when you asked them their own name they seemed scarcely able to remember it but referred to themselves by their service number and their friends by theirs. The camp staff tried to get them to use Christian names but failed. I wonder how many of them would have done service in the coming war.

Tuesday arrived and after an early lunch we set out. It seemed to me there were as many camp staff as there were boys. We got there quicker this time. Not having any drowning sheep to rescue. We were met at the gate by the lodge keeper who directed us to the path to the castle that we had used before, the steward was waiting at the castle and said his employer was not in residence and he would escort us. I though out camp commandant looked disappointed at not meeting the owner himself. There was some discussion about the condition of the ruins that it must have stood a siege. We disagreed and said in the civil war when castle owners knocked down the barbicans and blew out the floors to prevent their use by the enemy, but that was declared nonsense by some others. The steward led us through the gardens to the swimming pool. It was about half as big as the Victoria Park lido in the East End. Some of the party used the changing rooms and had a swim. I could not swim at the time so laid in the sun on one of the recliners.

The steward came to say tea was served and lead us back through the gardens to the servants' dining hall at the back of the house. I don't know how many servants they had but the table was at least eight meters long and with loaded cake stands down the middle and plates of sandwiches between and three servants down each side dressed in red coats, pantaloons, white stockings and shoes with big buckles and white gloves, and gold braid everywhere. Good job we had washed our hands. They started offering us sandwiches and pouring tea when the sandwiches were finished, they reluctantly I thought, started putting a selection of cake and pastries on our plates. The rest of the group began drifting away but I was daydreaming thinking perhaps I could be one of those servants, looking at all the cakes left and thinking about the chinaware on the dressers along the opposite wall. It was beautiful, with gold edges and fruit painted on them. You would not want to put your dinner on them. A sarcastic voice behind me said, 'Has Sir quite finished?' and a white gloved hand came round to take my plate. I growled and the hand disappeared. When I looked up I was the only one left and there were two servants standing each side of the door waiting to open it for me. I left my sixpence as a tip by my plate. I stood up and thanked him very much. He didn't look very pleased I thought, so I walked out - I can be sarky even if it cost me sixpence. 'There you are,' said one of the camp staff. 'Now you're here we will start our walk back.'

I spent the next few days fishing then back to the reality of trying to make some money in the East End.

Chapter 15   Uncle George's prediction

Luckily I had taken the precaution of telling my customers when I would be back and did not lose much trade. Hitler and his Nazis were still doing terrible things in Europe. He annexed Austria on the pretext that it was the will of the populace most of whom were Germany anyway and he wanted the return of the Sudatenland, taken from the Germans as reparations after what would be called the Great War. He also claimed the strip of land given to Poland, with whom we had a defence treaty. The population of this land was also predominantly German. Prime Minister Chamberlain went to see Hitler and on the 30th of September 1938 came back waving a piece of paper saying that he and Hitler had signed it to say there would be peace in our time.

Uncle George said, 'Hitler is not ready yet - and he will start when he is. It is to be hoped that our Government will start rearming.' Factories did start to get busier and there was a bit more money around but it was half hearted. Well Mr Hitler had promised peace in our time. The thinking seemed to be look at all the money wasted if there was no war, so we wandered on. Christmas came and went and through 1939 I carried on earning and the business was going well.

On Friday evenings Mum always answered the door as she was also selling cami-knicker sets and young ladies came to buy while they had their wages. There was a choice of colours, old gold, old rose, eau de nil (a sort of green), and blue. Their next stop was the public baths where, for sixpence, you got a nice hot bath and a bit of soap. A penny got you a packet of pine needles to scent the bath water. They then put on their new cami-knickers to meet the boyfriend and go dancing. Young men used to arrive at our door to buy new linen handkerchiefs for the top pocket of their suit jackets.

Eventually time passed and we began to forget the threat of war and we went on into 1939. The Government issued gas masks. Dad got and fitted ours and volunteered to deliver and fit masks on the housebound and bed-ridden old people and the all enclosing ones for babies and to teach mothers how to operate them. One young woman, when we tried to show her, went into a screaming fit as the baby was slid in and before it appeared in the transparent part was fighting us to pull it out again. Dad tried to explain why it was necessary for her to do it. All she kept on about was why did the Germans want to kill her baby. Dad said come on, we will leave this for now and come back later.

I must say I don't know how some of the bedridden would manage. They did not seem to comprehend what was happening to them and just stared out at us until we took it off again. Some almost suffocated, their breathing was so poor. Remembering in those days they had never seen a doctor or had medication of any kind. Plus most were still on gas lighting and the windows shut to keep warm. The only heating they had was either an open coal fire, or a paraffin heater if they could afford it, all adding their bit to the bad air quality. I did ask Dad how they would know if there was gas – he did not answer but he did solve the baby problem. He made a slightly larger baby with the head, arms and legs from an old doll and put a nappy on it and a dress. The young woman was quite happy putting the doll in and out of the respirator and then we hit another snag. She would not put her respirator on first. She was gong to save her baby first when Dad explained if she didn't put hers on first by the time she did the baby would suffocate because she would not be operating the pump. Dad did not say the other scenario, to use modern parlance, if she put the baby in and then got caught by the gas they would both die. Dad left her with an instruction pamphlet with simple plans showing the routine, and we left. Me - I just prayed there would be no gas. At twelve years old there did not seem there was much else you could do - I had all the horrors of gas instilled in me at age seven by Great Uncle George.

Life for me went on as normal – I was not doing so much firewood, now only for the family, and I carried on working at Bretts Saturdays and found another job helping to clean between the seats after the last act at The Queen Theatre Friday and Saturday evenings. This consisted of going up and down all the rows of seats with a sack picking up all the ice cream tubs and spoons, peanut bags and with an old dustpan, shovelling up most of the nut shells and other odds and ends - usually about two full sacks. Then the doorman and Buttons (a man dressed in a uniform with brass buttons all down the front) whose main job was to call the acts on stage at the right times, then vacuumed all through. I took to going early and helping Buttons by running down the corridors to the dressing rooms to call the acts.

As an indications of how down-at-heel and slightly-shabby everything was, Buttons' uniform was threadbare and the arms and legs seemed to be too short. Maurice Abrahams, one of the two brothers who were owners, asked me to ask Dad to call in and when he did he told Dad that the Buttons was retiring by the time I was fourteen and he would, if Dad agreed, give me the job of Buttons - with a new uniform. I suppose it was kind of him seeing that I was 'not going to be fit for anything much'. Dad had simply said there was time yet - but he would keep it in mind thank you. Just think - if the war had not come along I might have reached age seventy with a shabby uniform shrunk too short too.

There were all sorts of acts at the Queens Theatre – but to see elephants and lions in a theatre was amazing. When the circus came to the Queens they were preceded by a gang of men who came with great baulks of timber to strengthen the stage from below - to take the weight of the Elephants. The lions' travelling cages were parked up behind the Queens, where there was a large fenced-in space. They could also be 'spied on' by children looking through the slatted fence at the back and could be heard roaring at night from where we lived. As for the elephants, they were walked between the theatre and their 'lodging' at the stables belonging to the London, Midland and Scottish Railway down Blackwall Way. This meant they passed where we lived, always stopping to drink at the great granite horse-trough opposite our house, and often depositing foot-ball sized lumps of dung, which were hastily collected by keen gardeners.

One of the tabloid papers produced a map of Europe in its centre pages and small flags you could cut out and threadle on a pin to indicate whose army was where. There were English, Nazi and French flags. Dad pasted the map on some cardboard so we could keep track of events. The teacher at school, he who had lost his dinner, informed us a war was coming but we were not to worry because the one who got his tanks and planes there first would win. I, for one, thought we have had it then. Our army went to France no better equipped than in the Great War. I suppose the war office thought we had won the last war with this equipment so it would do this time - totally ignoring the high cost in men's lives - and the army dug in, after all it would be like last time wouldn't it? And nothing happened – we carried on business as usual.

Then my world turned upside down again as Hitler invaded Poland. Mr Chamberlain told him to desist and if he did not a state of war would exist between us.

SCHOOL MEMORIES

1939

Chapter 16 evacuation part one

On the morning of the second of September Mum told me to put my best clothes on and went with me to school. I don't remember being told I would be evacuated. She gave me a bag packed with my other clean clothes. I was told to get on the bus.

I wondered what I had done wrong. Mum just stood on the pavement looking up at me. Other lads were arriving and getting on. I never thought I would be reassured when I saw Jack Fairhead getting on. He sat by me – he was quiet and the others seemed subdued too, suddenly he blurted out that his Dad told him we were going to the country before the bombing starts. I looked out the window but Mum was gone. The bus took off, I told him what had happened to Carters dinner. He asked me why, I said it was because he'd whacked me round the legs and that was your (Fairhead's) fault – just so he knew where he stood.

We arrived at a railway station and eventually got on a train and that took off, after a while we had to get off and put our gear on the platform and were told not to wander off, so I stayed by my bag. I heard two teachers talking. One said, 'If they are trying to confuse Hitler they are doing a magnificent job,' and the other agreed.

Nearby there was a mountain of luggage with a big bundle of ballet shoes all tied by their laces and two service-looking ladies in pleated tweed skirts and they kept shouting things like 'Fiona stop pirouetting near the edge of the platform.' I looked round and there were 'Fionas' pirouetting all over the platform.

Finally we were put on another train which seemed to be stopping and starting frequently and at last arrived at the station, and were transferred to a coach, which finally deposited us at a sports pavilion at one end of a sport field. Once inside we were offered tea and bread and jam. We'd had nothing all day and the speed at which it disappeared sent some of them scuttling off to get more. There were other elderly ladies offering a sniff of sal volatile, the lads did not understand that and tried to drink it.

It seemed that there had been no arrangement made as to where we were to be lodged. I think they had been trying to find someone or somewhere and my sense of rejection increased.

Finally a group of us marched up the road to a double-fronted bungalow. We were taken in and the front room to the right was empty except for a carpet on the floor. We were given a blanket each and told to settle down for the night. Apart from our bag of clean clothes we had been given a paper carrier bag with some groceries in. I cannot remember now exactly what but mainly small tins of sardines or fruit, and condensed milk. My impression was that they were given to whoever was to look after us, so I did not touch mine neither did Jack.

We finally settled down, but there was quite a lot of noise going on. Suddenly the door burst open and a man shouted 'Keep quiet you lot!' and put the light out. In the morning we were told by the same man to get up and fold up our blankets and put them with our bags in the centre of the room. I folded my groceries in my blanket then went into the room opposite. I now realised we were in a café. They gave us a cup of tea and a slice of bread and jam each and sent us outside and told to 'make ourselves scarce' as the man put it. He pointed out an outside lavatory and told us to stay out of the house. It was plain that he did not want us there, so we wandered off.

He had two children who came out and showed us a small field out the back which had a small natural pond. So we played around until we were called by a smartly dressed lady who said that it had been arranged for the man to give us a dinner after his normal customers had left. Good job it was fine weather. We were duly called and by then we would have eaten anything, but I seem to remember it being enough.

After they said that Mr Chamberlain told Hitler he didn't withdraw from Poland by Midday a state of war would exist between us, or words to that effect. Hitler did not bother to answer so now it seemed we were at war, the date was now the third of September 1939 and we had just taken part in a mass evacuation of children from London. Our place of safety, after about six hours of waiting on stations and travelling by bus and train, was just 22 miles from home. I bet that fooled Hitler. My brother Peter went as far as Windsor.

That night, when we were allowed in, Jack and I were amongst the last in so we found a place on the opposite side of the room. The man appeared and shouted at us 'You brats, you spoilt my carpet with your condensed milk!' so while he was raging we rooted in our bags and showed him our unopened tins. That stopped him and then he said, 'I have had enough of you lot.'

It seemed to me that we were not wanted - so why were we there? I felt rejected and useless when I knew at home I was useful and earning. Eventually we were called together, collected our belongings and marched off to our new lodgings.

I was introduced to a young woman and she showed me up to a small room at the top of the stairs. It was nice, and she showed me the bathroom and disappeared. After a while I went down and out the back door and out the front gate to see where I was. The houses looked new semi-detached and in a crescent that started at the main road and swept round and rejoined to it. On the half circle of land opposite was the newly built pub on which the work seemed to have stopped and my billet was the third from the right.

As I had been dropped off first I did not see where the other boys went, so I went back in and went upstairs and through an open door. I saw the young woman nursing a small baby. Now I understood. I just sat on the bed until her husband came home - and decided I needed a bath. That was fair enough seeing as we had not been offered any washing facilities for three days. It seemed to me that they thought London boys became dirty very quickly as the bath routine continued every evening. He got tea ready and, apart from asking me where I came from, to which I replied London, I did not say East End as it seemed to frighten people, he didn't talk to me. After tea I asked if I could read the paper so I read until he suggested I should now go to bed. I slept alright, got up and had breakfast which Mr had prepared. I decided it would be alright so I gave him the groceries. After a few days I had a letter from Mum and Dad. I suppose they had been given my address. That was handy because until then I did not know where I was. They asked how I was and was it a nice billet? I wrote back yes to both. I did not say anything about the treatment we received. If my parents thought I should be here they must have a good reason. I took to washing up the breakfast things before the lady came down, I had the distinct impression that, not having older children, they did not know quite what to expect. I sometimes felt like a ghost wandering in and out.

One Sunday another young couple visited them and offered me a parcel. Puzzled I said thank you and just stood there not knowing what to do. I had never been given anything by complete strangers before so it was suggested I should take it to my room to see what it was. So I went and found it was two pairs of woollen underpants and two woollen vests. I went down and thanked them and not knowing what else to do I shook hands with them.

Half way into the next week two smartly dressed women came and called all evacuee lads together and marched us down the road to a small school, round the back of which was a small field, to be met by an elderly gentleman. I thought he must be the headmaster. Anyway he said he wanted this field dug for the 'dig for victory' and he explained how we were to double dig it so that the topsoil went underneath seemed a bit daft to us but we set to. Midday we were given some jam sandwiches and went to school in the afternoon.

Personally I learned little as the lessons were pitched below the standard of the eldest and too high for the youngest. I think they must have had more pupils than they could cope with as two ladies were constantly buzzing in and out.

Eventually we finished the digging and the head came out and said what a fine job we had done and so quickly too. Well I mean if country boys could do it, it would be dead easy for London lads, wouldn't it? So for a treat he took us off to see his chickens like we would not know what they were. I remember they were in large pens with a nice hen house in the middle and in each pen was a different breed - six hens and a cockerel in each. Apparently they were show birds. And there was I thinking they were for eating.

The other lads perked up as he explained that the four dwarf apple trees were not one variety - with a different variety in each pen. Quite a few of the lads were slow going home as they had not seen apples on trees before and closer inspection proved they came off in your hand quite easily. Needless to say, he was not too pleased next morning. Oh well, he did have his garden dug for nothing.

A few days later a lot of European Jewish children arrived and took over the girls' side of the school, and that made teaching and learning impossible. We tried to talk to them over the dividing wall in the playground, which was impossible because their command of English was confined to swear words which shocked even East End lads, who, amazing as it may sound, did not habitually swear. I can only think that someone thought it was funny to teach them to use such language.

One Sunday morning Jack met me and asked if I would walk with him to where his sister was billeted.

So off we went - well it was only nine miles. On our way we saw some big iron gates chained and padlocked with a soldier inside. We asked who lived there his reply was 'A treacherous Nazi. Now clear off.' We found out much later it was Oswald Mosley's estate and he was under house arrest. We had seen and heard him in the East End with his brown shirts bully boys, defying anyone to interrupt or heckle their boss.

Eventually we arrived at Jack's sister billet. She was with a young couple who were quite nice. They had already eaten, but they made us some sandwiches and talked to us for a while and they asked where we had walked from. We said and they suggested we should set off back as time was getting on.

When we arrived back there was a group of men on the green, the man I lodged with, among them. Someone shouted 'There they are!' and 'Where have you been?' and when we said, they seemed to have some difficulty believing it as apparently it was a good bit further than we thought. When we had not appeared for Sunday lunch they had been out searching - as London boys could get lost in the country. So we said we were sorry that we had not thought to say where we were going. They seemed glad to see us back safely. I thought perhaps they cared after all.

Jack and I still wandered about but made sure we would not be missed. So we went off one day to have a closer look at a large galleon type ship we had seen at a distance before. When we got there it was up on scaffolding and in a field beyond it we saw an Arab town all white with domes and towers and

Arabs walking about with arc lights shining on it even though it was daylight. Mystified we backed out and went home. We heard sometime later they were making the film, 'The Thief of Baghdad' at Denham Studios. I never saw the film. We were probably bombed out and gone to Devon by the time it came out.

Dad arrived one Sunday and chatted to the couple I was with, saying that he and Uncle Fred, Dad's half brother, who had an Austin Seven would take me down to Windsor to see Peter. He told me to get my jacket and as I left the room I heard him ask how I head been. So I hesitated thinking they might say I had disappeared. But no, they merely said I didn't say much, but everything was fine. So off we went and duly arrived at Peters billet where he and another boy lived with an elderly couple who called Peter Sunshine and the other one Chocolate. But they were both out fishing along Eton meadows, so we went to find them. We found them and spent a bit of time with them 'drowning worms' then took them home for tea and delivered me back to my billet before they headed home.

Chapter 17   evacuation two
– pillar to post

A few days later I was asked by someone if it was nice seeing my brother and I said about the fishing. Perhaps I should have kept quiet because a few days after that I was told that arrangements were being made to get us together. How I wished I had not said anything because the old couple at Windsor could not cope with another boy so Peter was brought to me and we were both moved to another house further along the crescent. This pair already had some evacuees. I never really knew how many. I did ask where we were to sleep and was shown upstairs to two rooms, one had two double beds in and the other, with no door, had one double. To get in you had to climb over the end. Where the couple and their small son slept I don't know.

The woman never cooked, my brother remembers it even today, there was a plate of jam sandwiches for breakfast, one of spam sandwiches for dinner and another of jam for tea. You were supposed to help yourself. There were no small plates so you had to get a handful, and in my case some for Peter. The other boys resented us for intruding and the bigger ones starting bullying, especially at mealtimes. I followed Dad's advice and dealt with it as before, and as before the bully went off whining. The lady soon told me she had put herself out to accommodate us and we should be grateful. As there had been no trouble until I came I must be the trouble-maker; obviously no-one had stood up to the bullies before. The bulling carried on in a different way –

sometimes all the sandwiches disappeared before I got there.

The lady of the house told us that she and her husband were a dance-act resting at the moment. Well I knew what resting meant – it meant they were not very good and could not get bookings. I suppose I was a bit daft, as I told her my parents ran a pro-house. Oh well!

He was a milkman and she taught dance, as a consequence there were girls there most evenings and you could not even get a bath without them crowding in - and the door lock was non-existent. So I took to staying out at night until they were gone. One evening it was raining so I stayed in only to find two or three girls tormenting Peter so I pushed them about a bit and they started to howl and Mr came in and said he had enough of me. The next day some lady I had not seen before came and said they were moving me out, but Peter would remain as the lady of the house thought he needed mothering. My thought was that she did not know the meaning of the word. Yet again I felt rejected.

I was moved round the corner to one of a pair of cottages, so old they had no mains drainage, just a bucket lavatory, and no running water. This couple had two children about Peter's age and the mother of one of the parents living there. That evening, after tea, the husband took me out for a ride in his van. He, I understood, was a milkman too and part of the job was running the bottling plant at night filling the bottles with milk for the morning delivery. I soon got the hang of it and helped putting the cardboard lids on and crating them and back to the cottage we went where they had fixed up a bed for me on the landing. They had put an enamel bowl of water in the oven for me to wash in; it smelt of burnt dinner. When I went to bed it did not feel dry but like one that had been slept in and not aired and smelt like it too. I was not happy, but my own actions had put me here so as the old adage goes 'as you make your bed you must lie in it'.

Next morning before I went to school I tried to help the children fetch water from the well in front of the cottages and shared by both cottages. The kids had a tin can about a gallon capacity (about four and a half litres) with a wire handle that you hooked on a pole and lowered down the well. It must have been ten feet or (three metres) deep - I promptly lost the can off the hook. The children ran off shouting that I had lost the can. Half the neighbours came out, or so it seemed, I had wiggled the pole about and regained the can but by so doing I had stirred up the sediments. Now until it settled nobody could use the water and that could take all day. So I went to school. It's hard to say how I felt but utterly useless came into it.

The morning dragged on with no gain. Reluctantly, it seems stupid now, but I did not want to go back to the cottage and I had not felt well all the morning. My head, arms and legs ached. We were still on half days so I missed dinner and went wandering in the woods instead and as the weather was damp my coat and trousers became wet so, miserable, I went back. They fussed around and put my coat and trousers in the over to dry and I spent the rest of the day laid on the bed still aching. When Mr came home I went down to a hot dinner. Nobody said anything much, so I returned to bed. And later that evening they called me down and seemed quite concerned and said they had a tablet for me to take. Well I tried and did not think to chew it first, so it took a lot of water to get it down. And they saw me to bed and laid something else on top. And I slept but as a consequence of all that water I wet the bed, something I cannot remember ever doing before! When I went down I told them what I had done and how sorry and disgusted with myself I was. They said I was not to worry about it as I had not been well, but the children were giggling.

When Mr came home he had bought a small leather purse for me. When they put my trousers in the oven they had noticed my money was loose in my pocket. I well remember that kindness, even after I spoilt the water and wet the bed. I did thank them - but if I had not then turned away and gone out I would have cried and that I was not able to face up to. The day dragged by and that night, when the house was quiet, I crept down the stairs to spend the night by the stove so as not to soil the bed again. To my surprise the Granny was there asleep in the armchair, so I just sat on a kitchen chair with my head on my arms on the table and when I heard movement upstairs I slipped back up to the bed, now knowing whose bed I had been occupying.

As it was Saturday and so no school I went round to find Peter, he said he was OK so we spent the day wandering in the woods, that night I repeated what I had done the night before. I felt bad about keeping the Granny out of her bed. Next morning, Sunday, I went round and stood on the green opposite Peter's billet waiting for him to emerge. An Austin Seven car drove into the crescent, stopped outside Peter's and Dad got out! He saw me and asked where Peter was. I pointed – he told me to wait and went in. When he came out with Peter and his clothes, the lady of the house was literally wringing her hands saying she had been given too many children to look after and she had not noticed what had been going on.

Dad put Peter in the car and turned to me and asked where I was staying. So I took him around to the cottage. On the way I told him about my wetting the bed and I had said sorry to the couple. When we went in Dad said he would be taking us home and sent me to fetch my gear. Dad apologised for my 'lapse' as he called it. They in turn said that I had been unwell. Dad gave them a ten shilling note, which I must say they would no take at first, but Dad insisted saying how he appreciated their kindness to me. Uncle Fred drove us home.

My parents knew I had been moved again on being sent my new address and apparently Mum said she was not having me moved about and told Dad to fetch us back. I was never asked what happened and very soon it seemed it never had. I do not suppose the whole sorry episode of our evacuation took much more than six weeks. And Mr Hitler had not fired a shot.

One thing I will add to the tale. Even now I still have to chew up tablets to wash them down. If only I'd thought to chew that earlier one I would not have suffered the embarrassment.

Chapter 18   home and work

On Monday morning Mum told me that Woolmore Street School was closed to be turned into a mortuary for the thousands of dead expected when the air raids started. So I went to Bretts and started full time – no-one said anything or asked where I had been. I still had the job, I supposed Brett thought I would be back when I was fourteen anyway, he said he supposed he would have to pay me full wage now. What a daft question. So I thought perhaps I could learn the grocery trade for a living, so apart from the shop cleaning, I also did stock rotation, where crates of tin goods were always being turned over (re-stacked) so new were at the bottom and the old on top. I don't suppose health and safety would allow fourteen year olds to lift those weights today.

Dried fruit was sold loose those days and came to the warehouse in big boxes. Before they were offered for sale they were washed and steamed to plump them up and make them shine, and samples were laid out in shallow trays so the customers could choose what they wanted. Various types of rice came in two-hundred weight sacks, i.e. 224 pounds which is, I suppose, something like 100 kilos. As the shop called for more it was put in a drum and turned until it polished itself and so on. The work filled the day and the call for this or that commodity was continuous. My full pay for five and a half days was the magnificent sum of seven shillings and six pence which would equate today to about thirty pounds.

Of course working full time I could no longer do my other earners. I still did bundles of firewood on my half days and that was easier because I had exclusive rights to the crates from the shop which were broken up and taken home each evening. One Monday on my way I stopped to look in Wells' shop window to see if there was anything interesting. I did hear a horse and cart behind me, that was nothing unusual, then suddenly there was a clatter of hooves and a shout, the horse crashed over and I was trapped against the window! Somebody said, 'Keep still lad' as if I could do anything else. I could see in the reflection in the window a man sitting on the horses head and its legs were thrashing about and someone came running and in a minute the movement ceased.

I was helped to climb out over the horse. The farrier I used to talk to had cut its throat and the blood was running along the gutter. The farrier said it had a 'colic seizure'. I set off again, running, otherwise I might have been late for work. As I was sweeping through the shop a lady customer came in all of a dither and upset. She had seen a horse fall over on a boy and the blood was all over the place. She suddenly said, 'That's the boy!' so I slipped out of the back until she had gone. I was afraid they might have thought it was my fault.

Soon after that Mum had a letter, it seemed that the education authority realised that a lot of children, for various reasons, had returned and as we were not yet fourteen we had to return to school, so now once again it was half days and especially for my inconvenience it was to be afternoons at a school the other side of the East India Dock Road, with the usual resentment of the pupils whose school it was, some of whom held back to sort us out. Unlike the Denham lads these were East Enders and of course fights took place and teachers came running to separate us. Of course us 'incomers' were blamed, with the headmaster declaring he could not wait for us to become fourteen so that peace could reign once more. For me, personally, it was further rejection.

Most of us had been working and were losing money for no educational gain: just to keep some pen pushers books straight. The teachers were ineffective – we were not writing essays or doing any arithmetic except a bit of mental-maths - I don't believe they were even real teachers. The one we had used to waste our day telling us tales about motoring in the highlands and about having to sweep up grit with his hands to make the drive belt grip and the trauma of hearing the carburettor boil over because of the altitude. For an East End boy the idea of lying in the road sweeping up grit was stupid. Try that on the East India Dock Road. If a tram didn't get you then a copper would.

Eventually we received our bit of paper telling us we were fourteen and were legit, accompanied by a big sigh of relief from the headmaster. I went back to Bretts and started work. Yet again I did not think to ask if someone else had got the job. Brett was in his office and didn't seem to notice. The girls arrived – I said good morning and they replied. It was just like I had not been away. I did wonder what happened when I was not there ... and life strolled on.

A Chinaman came in the shop one day and asked to see Brett and was invited in to the office. When he came out Brett walked to the door with him and stopped by me and said, 'Do you know the Chinese café in Ming Street?' I knew it - well there was only the one. I used to look in their dustbin often as I used to collect food tin labels from around the world and they had all sorts of weird things like water chestnuts. Brett said, 'I want you to take a sack of rice there.' So down in the cellar I went and he had marked a sack. Well I wrestled the sack upstairs, which took a while - well weighing 224 pounds it was twice my body weight. I eventually got it up to the shop. Brett came out of his office and said, 'It's a bit late now – take it tomorrow.' I never knew whether he thought I should have got it up quicker but I thought 'good show' as I felt I was not in a state to go straight away as it must be at least a mile with a sack barrow and the full weight of the sack and barrow hanging on your arms. I had forgotten the road was cobbled and it would have been illegal to take it on the smoother pavement so next morning after cleaning and bringing in what the shop needed I set off with the rice up out of Chrisp Street over the crossing on the East India Dock Road, turned towards Lime House. That was when I remembered the cobbles round the Easton pub and down West India Dock Road to Ming Street and then had to strain to get the barrow up on the pavement as it was higher than the wheel centres. I managed it finally.

The café door was open so I pushed the barrow right up to it, and the Chinaman appeared and started to pull the sack off and to the right. I leaned over the barrow to see where he was putting it. The inside of the café was gloomy but I could just see a few Chinese eating using chopsticks and two English women sitting talking, then suddenly to my left there was squealing scream and a door banged open and a younger Englishwoman came running out crying and a Chinaman following her. One of the other women jumped up and got in the man's way, put her hands on his chest and speaking Chinese pushed him back in the room. Needless to say I was transfixed by the proceeding and had not noticed the customer had come back and was standing in front of me. He saw he had my attention and, with a hissing noise, he drew his finger across his throat. The result was a record breaking run with a sack barrow, straight down Poplar High Street and left through the recreation ground, with the keeper shouting 'you can't race through here with a barrow like that!' I was gone, dodging the traffic as I crossed West India Dock Road down Chrisp Street, through the shop and out the back into the warehouse. Brett came out and said whatever possessed you to charge through the shop like that. I told him I thought the girls might be waiting for me to bring in some stock. He shook his head and went back into his office.

Another job that I had was to deliver the parcels of groceries that the lady customers ordered and collect the money and sign the receipts 'with thanks'. To deliver them Brett had a cart; if you can imagine like a small sedan chair on wooden iron-rimmed wheels and wooden shafts. Well the whole thing was rickety and remember the cobbled road, pulling it along was like holding onto two jack-hammers. Well one morning I set out up Chrisp Street across East India Dock Road turn left towards

Aldgate and just then the air-raid sirens went and people started hurrying along to the shelter under St Georges Hall. A police sergeant was standing there chivvying the people to hurry on down and when he spotted me he shouted out 'Down here lad'. I said, 'I have a load on' and he said, 'Don't worry about that, I'll keep an eye on it'. I mean, me - trust a copper to keep an eye on it? So I said, 'Ok Sergeant. Just then there was several bangs over Stratford way and he disappeared inside - so much for keeping an eye on it. I was back between the shafts and away.

When I finished the round and got back and handed the money in Brett said did you find shelter somewhere. I said, 'No why?' He said, 'During the raid.' I looked puzzled and said, 'What raid?' He muttered something and then said, 'You're tuppence short,' and stopped it out of my wages. I used to wonder which of the lady shoppers had my tuppence; so after that I always checked their money before I got back and was surprised to find sometimes I was up, so used it to top up when I was down. I thought that probably some of those superior ladies were no better at counting than me.

There was a young man who used to have a stall in the market and sold cheap cosmetic stuff, scented soaps and hair shampoo, all the usual stuff and of course the girls used to crowd around and he had a line of banter that kept them laughing. But his drawback was he was not only just five foot tall but five foot round with it. One Saturday an old Aunty was looking after his stall and when asked she said he had 'gone for a solider'. And of course the usual comment was we must be worse off for soldiers than we thought.

A good while later there was a commotion down the market; girls were leaving their stalls and greeting a solider striding up the street. It was the cosmetics lad. He had joined the Cornish Light Infantry, the fastest marching regiment in the British Army, and there he was lean as a whippet, chest out, shoulders back, head up, and as smartly turned out as a guardsman. He gave his aunty a hug, took over the stall and practically sold out in an hour with all the market girls buying stuff just to have a chat. I wonder if he survived. I never saw him there after the War.

Chapter 19   bombing raids

Jerry had been a nuisance all the following Friday and some people were not bothering to shelter despite air raid wardens running about blowing their whistles. I worked in the shop and customers came in each with a tale about the previous night's raids and the damage they had seen and the casualties. I ran home lunchtime to see if I had a home; everything was all right so then ran back to work.

There was a barrage balloon in All Saints church graveyard and when it went up so did all the others. They must have had only one telephone between them. Jerry kept us awake all night and Saturday morning I set off for work taking detours because of delayed action bombs left to keep us busy until he came back. We opened the shop and the market was getting ready. There was a clear blue sky and we were busy then around three o'clock the sirens went and, unlike other days, the customers cleared and the stallholders packed up, as if there was a universal premonition. Brett said close the shop – we stood outside watching the vapour trails of the dogfights between RAF fighters and German fighters trying to destroy the RAF so their bombers would have a clear field.

A police woman came up the street, the first I had seen, and as she went by one of the sons of the wet fish merchant next door gave a long whistle and slammed his hand down on the stall - Bang! She stopped, turned around and walked straight for them and ordered them inside, and these two hulking great lads went in like little children.

A real bomb landed behind the shop, on the opposite side of the road, by the time all the staff got through the wicker door, I was last and the cellar flap was closing. I pulled out a dried fruit bin from under the counter and crawled in the space. Several more bombs exploded in Chrisp Street and shook stuff off the shelves. When the raid eased up I came out and stood on the cellar flap and shouted I'm off home - and to my relief it was still there.

The sirens went often as Jerry was now concentrating on our air defences and civilians were spending their nights in their shelters. Dad's sister Bess, who lived with us, could not negotiate the blast wall and descent into our shelter, because from the age of five she was a polio victim and had to wear a leg iron which restricted her mobility, so Dad got permission for her to use the shelter that was built by a local firm in their warehouse. This shelter had been built for the office staff of the firm and as the firm had moved their head office to Reading it was unused. It was well built and the access tunnels were zigzagged to stop blast and the whole covered with a thousand tons of asbestos in two hundred weight sacks – really safe and snug. One night Jerry decided it was our turn and because we sat between the East India Docks and Millwall Docks we were in the target zone and as we sat in our shelter we could feel the concussion of the bombs through the soles of our shoes and then we got an extra hard thump which lifted the concrete floor.

Sometime later Dad came and told us a hole had been discovered in the garden behind our shelter and that the man in his shelter said he had been shook off his seat by his shelter jumping up, luckily for us it was a large delayed action bomb so everyone was got out of their shelters and moved up the road to the shelter where Aunt Bess was, but in reality less than seventy yards away, around thirty people were brought in including children. After a couple of hours there was some muttering – 'we would be more comfortable in our own shelter' but half past one we got the answer. The bomb's clock set it off and the bang rattled my teeth. The lights went out and we sat in shock. When the emergency lights came on we were all covered in white dust with it piled on our heads - nobody knew about the dangers of asbestos in those days! While we waited for a lull in the raid we set about cleaning up ourselves and Dad came in and told Mum 'Jerry has gone home for another load' and we were to move to a surface shelter down a road opposite, called Ditchburn Street, which went gently downhill, levelled out and the climbed up to Preston Road.

So we set out - delayed action bombs were still keeping air raid wardens and the fire brigades busy. Dad went in front clearing debris out of the way, so with Mum in front carrying Dorothy, then me helping Aunt Bess, whose leg iron made progress slow and traumatic, even with me supporting her and holding the belt on the back of Mum's coat to steady her and all the while shrapnel was slashing down off to our left and Aunt Bess going on about 'was her furniture alright' because she had heard Dad tell Mum we had lost the house which meant we had lost our business and my future employment.

We made it to the shelter and Dad said it's a bit wet in there - which was a gross understatement there must have been at least couple of inches of water in there and it smelt of urine. Dad found something for Mum and Aunt Bess to sit on. I bent my knees and leant against the wall. Peter leant against me. I have no idea how many were in there as it was pitch dark, there was a small glow now and again, someone was smoking. Aunt Bess was still moaning: the seat was too tall and hard and then Jerry came back and every time a bomb dropped the water rippled across the floor and slapped up the wall and back again.

Occasionally a bomb would whistle coming down and some woman moaned and someone said you 'Don't have to worry love you won't hear the one that gets you' and someone replied and 'If it shuts your stupid mouth at the same time we will all be happy.' I believe that was typical East End black humour. Eventually it became light and Jerry went home. After all it's one thing bombing us in the dark and another staying around when the anti aircraft guns and our fighters could see them.

When they were coming by day and sending bigger squadrons the hurricanes and spitfires knocked down one hundred and forty-four or one gross as the newspapers put it. As we came blinking out of the shelter and up Ditchburn Street it was easier to see the debris but it was still difficult for Aunt Bess; at the corner there was a body lying against the brick filled wall covered with some old coats, and the blood had run across the pavement into the gutter. Someone asked the young policeman who it was and he said, 'A woman and she's not been identified yet.'

A fire engine came up the road from Blackwall stairs and the crews faces and hands were black with soot and two were laid out on the top - collapsed with heat and exhaustion. One asked Dad if there was the chance of a cup of tea. Dad said, 'Sorry mate there's no water but there is a WVS van down Robin Hood Lane' so off they went. They had been fighting fires for all of twelve hours and we were unable to give them a cup of tea.

Now we could see our house – the whole row was standing. I looked and thought we're all right until I realised all the curtains were hanging outside and four front doors were open including ours. When we arrived at the house I helped Dad clear the glass and debris off the steps to the front door. He pushed the door and frame back in, unlocked the door and went in. After a while he came out and told Mum it was quite safe in the passage so we went in. Aunt Bessie's room was in a mess but soon Dad brought a bowl of water he had drained out of the boiler in the basement scullery and some food from the larder. Mum, Dorothy and Aunt Bess used the water to have wash while Dad, Peter and me went out the back door and down the stairs to the garden. Our shelter was tipped towards the house and the sides were squeezed in. Had we stayed we would not have survived that. The garden wall behind the hen run was down but the roost was only part demolished. When I helped Dad pull the side away there was only one partly feathered traumatised hen left - Dad killed it as it would have died anyway. Immediately behind the rubble was the edge of the crater, which was at least thirty meters across judging by the remains of garden walls. The next two shelters had disappeared and the third over was partly bent on the far edge of the crater and squeezed even flatter than ours. The reason there was no water was that the crater was rapidly filling up. We looked back towards the house. I remembered my tortoises but they had not survived the blast.

These houses where originally built for ship owners and captains in the eighteen hundreds and, of course, bricked up with mortar and had a window to light the staircase up three floors. The blast had peeled the walls back each side widening as it got higher and we could see the furniture hanging there. We went back in through the basement door which, because it was below ground level, was undamaged. Dad retrieved some more tinned food – there was no fresh meat or fish as there were no fridges back then and a deep freezer was just a vague promise for the future. Mum had stripped Aunt Bessie's bed and with some clothes tied up in a sheet plus what she could safely get from their bedroom and out onto the pavement we went. Uncle Fred arrived with a small van borrowed from his employers. We loaded our salvaged possessions and set off. Nothing had been said but I began to realise there *was* a plan B. Uncle Fred had been on this firm's telephone finding out what railway stations were still operating. I spent the journey bracing myself against the side to keep Aunt Bess from falling off the bedding bundle as she couldn't climb up into the cabin front or sit on the floor, or, when we stopped, helping Dad clear debris only to be sent back by a policeman because of delayed action bombs. He asked where we were going and he told us the way we could possibly get through.

We seemed to be making progress when the van stopped and I could hear Dad talking but I could not see as there were no windows and Aunt Bess was moaning about how stuffy and smelly it was. So I opened the back door and dropped out leaving the door open. Dad was talking to a high-ranking policeman. Dad had been asking him if there was anything he could do. I saw across the road the side of a block of flats had blown out and they were getting out the dead and injured and it seemed there were a lot more dead than living. When he saw me he asked Dad who he had in the van. Dad said my family and as soon as I have them away safe I'll be back and he said, 'Good man' and accepted Dad's first aid kit.

I jumped in and shut the door and Aunt Bess said my hands were hurting her shoulders. I wanted to scream at her to shut up – there were people dying out there. But I could not – she was frightened and vulnerable so I buried the scream in my mind where it has lodged for seventy years only to burst forth now.

Queen's Hotel
Repton
August 24th 1940

Many thanks for making us
comfortable in spite of the
stress. We very pleased to
return, and shall certainly
recommend.

Best of luck.
Sincerely yours
Mr & Mrs R. Evans

Queen's Hotel
August 31, 40

Many thanks for
a comfortable week.
excluding Jerries'
Air Raids

Jack Thompson

The last entries in the Guest Book before & Blackwall Way
was damaged beyond repair by bombing in the Blitz

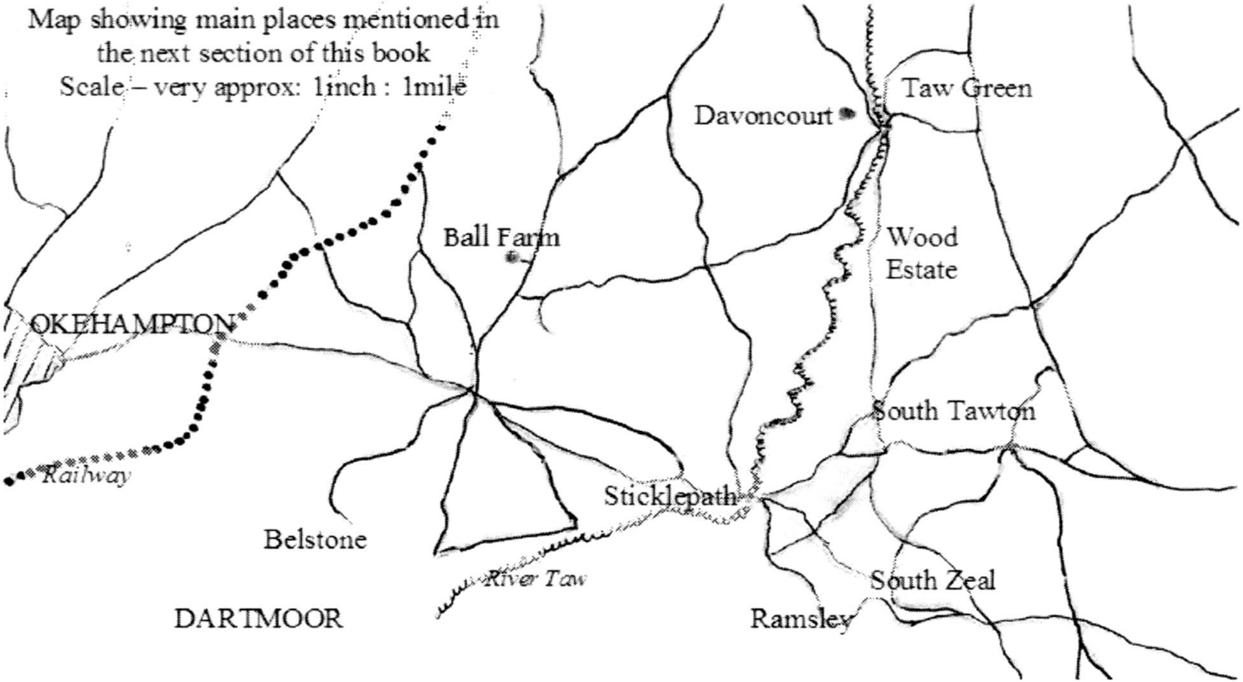
Map showing main places mentioned in
the next section of this book
Scale – very approx: 1inch : 1mile
Davoncourt
Taw Green
Ball Farm
Wood
Estate
OKEHAMPTON
South Tawton
Railway
Sticklepath
Belstone
River Taw
South Zeal
DARTMOOR
Ramsley

Chapter 20   down to Davoncourt

We finally arrived at Charing Cross – the ticket office told Dad that there would be a train to the West but the direct lines West were out of commission so this train will connect to a North West line but we may have to change at some point so, while we waited, we got some tea and buttered buns for Mum and Aunt Bess. Mum opened a tin of sardines that were among the tinned stuff we had salvaged. It was now Midday and they hadn't had anything since just before the bomb went off - I remember that because Aunt Bess said. I wondered why she didn't realise nothing would ever be the same again. We were refugees.

With much shunting and backing up and delays where men were working on the lines we finally found we were moving West and on through the night. And as the sky began to lighten I began to recognise stations.   We finally arrived at Okehampton around five in the morning, got off the train and, complete with our great bundles of bedding, moved into the waiting room. The station was deserted except for a station master who I believe thought we were gypsies.   Mum soon enlightened him – he said we would not get a taxi until about six.   Anybody that has been to Okehampton would know that it lies in a deep valley but the station is high above on the edge of the moors and at that time in the morning was bitterly cold; even colder than the train carriage. I expected Aunt Bess to complain but her face was grey and strained. I think she had come to realise the state we were in. Just before we had got on the train Dad said to me that he knew I would take care and help Mum as much as possible but it would be difficult and hard but we would get through it. And the family would come together again. He was to stay in London working and carrying on with his air raid warden's duties happy in the knowledge that we were safe. I just nodded.

Eventually a taxi arrived and I asked him to wait while I fetched Mum. Mum came out and he agreed to take us to Aunt Betts; who was a cousin of Mum's. At last I thought I knew where we were going. It had to be Taw Green Mill where I stayed as a child. The driver kindly helped get Aunt Bess in and out the taxi, Mum carrying Dorothy, Peter and the small baggage, but came back for me and the big bundles of bedding. As we travelled out the taxi driver said, 'On the wireless they had said London was in flames and fallen houses.' I could only nod and then he said, 'Did you see many dead people lying about.' I went stiff and could not speak and stared at him and he said, 'Oh, I'm sorry lad only they do talk such nonsense on the wireless.'

I was wondering why we had not turned off onto the road to Taw Green, we were heading for Whiddon Down, but he pulled across to a bungalow on his offside opposite Liverton Lane. Aunt Bett had married and now lived there with her husband who was a market gardener and rabbit trapper - catching upwards of three hundred a night which were gutted, boxed up and put on the train for London by six every morning. What with his couple of acres of gardens and poultry and picking up and relocating his traps I don't know how he slept. In the weeks we were there he never said much but trailing him I learned quite a bit about trapping - which later helped me to feed the family. There was no myxomatosis then so it was all clean and healthy meat. At that time I did not know that we were waiting for a cottage at Taw Green to be cleared. Nobody had lived there for years and consequently was used as a store for old farm junk. During this period Dad and his brother-in-laws and some friends were retrieving whatever they could from the house getting to the upper floors with ladders bringing down the lighter furniture and the lighter modern beds, the cutlery, crockery, cooking utensils, my prize books, and the family's, eventually they had a large van full and by that time Davoncourt had been cleared. (pronounced DeevonCourt)

Mum wrote to Dad that we were ready. He arranged for a van and an arrival date was set. On the due date mid-morning we set out for Davoncourt. I don't know how far it was now. But because Aunt Bett's bungalow was on the highest stretch of the road Okehampton to Exeter Road from where, if the weather was good, you could see the blue sparkle of the sea on the north Coast, and the cottage was near the river Taw which is the only river from Dartmoor flowing North, the trip was all downhill - probably five miles. When we got there Aunt Bett went back to guide the van down – we settled down but there was only one old chair. Aunt Bess sat down and we had a few sandwiches saving some for Dad and the drivers. Aunt Bess said how good it would be to sleep in a bed again.

But the time gradually passed and I had to go to the river to get some water to prime the pump outside, which was the water supply, so we could make some tea. I soon learnt to keep a bucket of water in the cottage, especially when the winter came when I would leave it on the stove so as to prime and thaw it out at the same time. Aunt Bess was not happy to find the lavatory was a hole in a board over a bucket twenty yards away. And still the van did not arrive and it began to get dark, so I tried to get a fire going. The farmer had put a few logs in. Aunt Bett was going to bring an oil lamp and the bedding down on the van. I started a fire in the stove but quickly had to put it out because it smoked so badly so I lit it in the inglenook instead. Peter helped, Dorothy was as good as gold. As you can imagine it is difficult to get big round logs to catch fire without a lot of kindling so I went out into the barn to see what I could find, or rather what I could feel to find, and got a piece of board with two legs one end badly worm eaten took it in and good old woodworm helped me to smash it and in no time had a nice fire which Aunt Bess promptly sat right in front of.

The room warmed up but because nobody had lived there for years the one metre thick cob walls, that is clay with wisps of straw reinforcing and a thatched roof, held a lot of cold. With it getting colder outside the fire had a lot to do. We settled down for the night Aunt Bess on the chair. Mum found a big towel in the small baggage to wrap around Dorothy, who was only four at the time, and with her on her lap one side of Aunt Bess I sat the other side with Peter. And Aunt Bess said, 'We should have stayed at Betts even if we were sleeping on the floor. I thought I would sleep in a bed tonight.' I wondered why she did not realise they may have got caught in a raid and will never come, but before I could explode Mum pointed at the fire – it was getting low. Open hearth fires are hard to control like a bonfire there is no draught or flue control. I said, 'Sorry Mum it will go out anyway - we have no more wood.'

When dawn came to revive us we could barely stand up to move around to relieve the cramp got from sitting on the cold flagstone floor. I went into the barn and found some more wood and then I went to get some milk from the farm. The farmer's wife, Mrs Penwarden, gave me a jug of milk and half a loaf of bread and a small bowl with a lace cover with beads hanging round the edge and refused my offer of money. Mum soon boiled some milk and Dorothy had bread and milk. Mum, Peter and I had a thick slice of this lovely home-made bread with a big dollop of clotted cream on top. I had read about manna from heaven and came to the conclusion it must have been clotted cream! Aunt Bett said she did not want any of that milk as it was raw it hadn't been pasteurised. I did know about Pasteur – he stopped some sheep from dying and I'm absolutely certain he hadn't boiled them. Mum said, 'Well all the more for us then,' and then the question came from Aunt Bess 'What's that cream like then?' Mum looked at me and said, 'Definitely unpasteurised!'

I started to take the flue pipes off the range and after a bit of lifting parted it from the range – it seemed to pass up through a slot about 8 ft or 2m - the flue was clear. Then the farmer came with his daughter. I suddenly wished I wasn't so dishevelled and dirty and wanted to hide. He'd spotted the fire and said he had brought up a faggot, which was the name for a large bundle of dry kindling that they used to boil a kettle. Mum told him we had used some old wood from the barn – he replied that anything in there we could use, he just hadn't found time to burn it up. Then he saw me and said, 'You don't want to bother with that boy it's never been any good.' I had wriggled my hand down the flue outlet and feeling around and I touched something soft and furry. Well my hand shot out of there on its own; my elbow hit the wall and skin came off - and with her standing there smiling I could not look at it or give it a rub. He said, 'What did you jump like that for?' I wished he would take her away - I was experiencing some disturbing reactions. I carried on trying to move the obstruction with a piece of wire and finally pulled out a mummified barn owl! I then put the flue back. Mum came over with some paper kindling and we lit the fire - it did not smoke and mum said quietly to me, 'Margaret is twenty years old.'

Oh well, perhaps the age gap was a bit big (she still lives or did last Christmas when we always exchange cards and news. She did marry and is now a widow and is ninety-two whereas at the time of writing this I am eighty-five and my wife of fifty-eight years is eighty-one). A short time after they left we heard a hooter from down the lane. The lorry had arrived! Dad, the lorry driver and mate got out and Aunt Bet. Dad introduced Mum. The driver said, 'They ain't gonna find you down here Mrs. I think this lady (Aunt Bett) thought I was driving an Austin Seven,' and they started to unload.

I was amazed at what had been salvaged and, knowing Mum would not have registered anywhere for rations yet, the shops being at South Zeal - a walk of at least five miles, they had brought tea, sugar, potatoes, a cabbage and a leg of lamb. Mum looked at Dad and said, 'Where?' But the driver cut in with 'Don't ask Mrs,' - I just assumed it had 'fallen off the back of a lorry'. So Mum said how much coal have you found. Dad said they had retrieved about five hundred weight - around two hundred and fifty kilos of coal - so the range was soon going and Mum was roasting the leg using a bit of butter and the spuds and cabbage and by the time the unloading was finished and groceries unpacked, cutlery laid out, the chairs arranged we all sat down to a nice dinner. The driver announced it was the best meal he had since his Mrs had evacuated. Of course with seven adults, counting myself, and two children there was not a lot of the lamb left.

The lorry left with Dad. Aunt Bett had told them of an easier route back to the road for Exeter and she stayed to help put up the beds, she had also brought down some paraffin and an oil lamp and I had found an old hurricane lantern in the barn so now the cottage was getting warm and there would be light tonight. After Aunt Bett left and Peter and Dorothy were asleep, Aunt Bess went to her room, which was on the right as you went in the front door as there was no way she could get up the stairs as they were very narrow and started at right angles to the flight before they turned, in five steps, to be inline. Mum started to tell me the cause of the lorry delay and there was a shout from Aunt Bess. We went in thinking something really terrible had happened but, on having taken her boots off, she found the flag stones cold to her feet so just when we thought we settled down and talked we had to start unpacking boxes that we were going to leave until tomorrow to find her bed-side rug. Rug found; Aunt Bess happy, I said to Mum 'So what happened?' but she said we have both had enough for today so to go to bed. 'But I will tell you not to worry if you can't find a job, we will manage.' So I just said, 'I will go and get a bucket of water from the pump to prime it with tomorrow morning.' Thinking 'I *will* find something.' I could not bear the thought of being a liability.

Mum sitting in the porch of Davoncourt

Chapter 21   learning the farming ropes

Once again there were no jobs for London boys. Most of the farms were small and the farmers had their own sons. So I made myself useful around the place. I had to fix up a bucket lavatory in the corner of the scullery because Aunt Bess declared she could not be expected to go down that rough old garden path especially at night because you never knew what was out there. I scoured the land all around for every bit of fallen wood, half the time not knowing whose land I was on. I saw a man one day throwing turnips up into a cart so I joined in – he said nothing but when the cart was full he came round and said, 'I suppose you're that London boy from Davoncourt?' I gave him a nod. He then said, 'I have a job for you - dung-spreading.' I said thank you. He then told me what it involved and he would pay me for what I managed to do. He said turn up at seven and I will get you started and he picked up two nice turnips gave them to me and went on his way. I went home thinking what's so difficult about spreading a bit of dung about.

I was moving by half past five, brought in wood, primed the pump, took two buckets of water in, emptied Aunt Bess's bucket and was on my way. The farmer met me and we went to the field and there were piles of dung in perfectly straight rows at twelve paces apart, both ways, there was already a man working there. The instructions were to spread the dung in six by six face squares. Plain enough, the other worker was getting a fork full swinging up about forty five degrees and shaking it and the dung scattered evenly so I started to do this as well.

The dung fork (dung evils), for starters, was five toed on a shaft at least six feet long and almost too thick to close my hand around. The next snag was that dung is not a consistent material, ranging from sloppy half-rotted straw to great lumps of brown to black cheese. The first forkful pointing in the right direction was swung up and shaken - except it stayed on the fork as I shook it. I quickly came to the conclusion that farm work was nothing like the grocery trade. After I got three heaps done, the other man came over and said, 'Bait time boy.' (break-time) I didn't have anything so I said, 'I'll carry on.' He then said, 'Master won't like they big lumps left.' I looked at him and asked how I was supposed to cut them up. He took my fork and swung it about two inches off the ground and they seemed to slice up and scatter. That was simple enough. I swung at one – it stayed where it was and the shaft whacked me across the ribs. I did get better at it and managed six heaps. As I went home my arms and shoulders were saying I should have stopped at three and my thighs and stomach muscles were in full agreement; I went home slower than I came.

Mum had bought some farmhouse bacon and if you have never met it, it is about a centimetre and a half of meat with about eight centimetres of fat and about three centimetres thick, she had roasted it with potatoes and some of those turnips. Mum said there was plenty as Aunt Bess had said if this was living in the country she would sooner face the bombing. To me it was as good as I had ever had. Mum, who never missed a trick, announced she was going to make an early night as she had walked to

South Zeal and back to register the ration books. Really she only wanted to get me to go to bed without actually saying so. I was more than glad to comply. Next morning however was a different story. Stiff? I wondered whether I'd ever move again! But a few tentative star jumps and a bit of a trot down the lane eased things and I got there a bit early and started, the other man arrived and stood staring and hauled out his watch.

Well I got three more done by the time the farmer arrived. He came over to me and said Old Steven had told him I would not be there today. I thought 'how simple they are. I was owed money, of course I would be there.' He then said Steven would finish off now and gave me one shilling and sixpence. I thought here we go – paid off, got the sack, born useless. He pulled a small bottle from his pocket and said, 'Here lad rub this into your shoulder and arm and anywhere else that's stiff but don't get it near your privates!' I was mystified – sacked one minute and given medication the next - or was it some joke at my expense? But his next words were to 'Come Saturday evening and go down to the chapel. The farmers and their families will be there and you will get more casual.' I went home thinking these Devon people were a lot of yoyos. You did not know whether they were up or down.

I gave Mum the one and six, did some odd jobs that came easier now some tools had come down. I went in the barn, got stripped off, started to rub the liniment in, or that was what it said on what was left of the label. I put my clothes on and it started to warm up and went in almost immediately, Aunt Bess got up muttering 'If I have got to put up with that stink I am off to bed.' Mum had done a nice thick stew but after a few coughs from the others I took mine out in the barn, besides I needed to be there to remove my trousers. I had rubbed some of the stuff on my thighs and it was getting where he warned me not to get it. I slept in the barn, got up early, went down to the river and sat in it until things cooled down.

I did get offered work; somehow word had got around that the London boy was a worker. I have one of those 'dung evils' here at Radland, left by the previous owner, so I measured it and is seven foot long (two meters thirty) and weighs three kilos or six pounds nine ounces. I did hear later that nobody would have given that job to a boy – as it was a man's job.

As summer wore on jobs were coming in spasmodically. One evening a foreman asked if I would do 'something' I just looked at him and he suddenly said, 'It is not dung spreading, it's cutting me a lot of hazel rods. I will show you how and I know you already know all the hedgerows for miles around.' Apparently a thatcher was coming to tidy up his roof. (Hazel rods had to be straight between two and a half and five centimetres thick and were split down by the thatcher and twisted into thatching spears and when finished were sharp bent like a staple thirty centimetres long.

In those days farmers cropped their hedges for fuel and only did a section of hedge every six or seven years to give him a range of fuel from faggots up to logs anything from three to ten centimetres in diameter. So it was easy to tell at a distance what hedges would yield what you wanted, simple, so he gave me this bill hook. Well I knew about them – they were adapted from a medieval weapon and when mounted on a long pole could chop a knight off his horse so a bit of wood would not be any bother. I found my first rod, a beauty so keeping my left hand away I took a swipe and bramble, with malice afore thought, wrapped itself around my wrist. The jerk made the bill hook leave my hand and, spinning past my head, it stuck in the ground five meters away. Lesson one; clear the brambles away and take small chops. I unwrapped the bramble from my wrist and stopped the blood dripping out with my handkerchief, retrieved the bill hook and successfully detached the rod from the hedge.

By the time it was getting dark I had as much as I could carry. The farmer met me and reckoned he wanted as much again, he said, 'Come tomorrow and I will show you how to recognise farm boundaries.' Well that was me told. I mean what's a stick or two between farmers. But it seems they were jealous about their boundaries. I was told later, they said, 'What could anyone expect from that London boy?'

The next job I got was turning hay, there were seven others in the field - all women. I thought somebody was thinking that was all I was fit for, hay turning, which was done by hand as there was not a machine to do it those days. If there was, these farmers never had one and the only person who had a tractor was Aunt Bett's husband. I thought if I could not beat the ladies at this it would be a poor thing, after all it was only dried grass in rows; that was until I was given a pitch-fork - two steel rods slightly curved eighteen centimetres apart on a hundred and fifty two centimetres pole. Now they were really joking. But the ladies were getting it done and talking all the time no concentration at all. Just slipping the fork under the hay and flip it over.

I know why they had given me mine because it had a will of its own fifty per cent of the time it just stuck in the ground and I was falling behind. Finally one woman came back and showed me how to slide it under the hay, by sliding under the hay with the curves on the ground it kept the tips off the ground. I did thank her but I asked her why she had not instructed me in the first place. She said, 'Being as you're a London boy we thought you would know.' I said, 'In London we use these things for sticking in one another. Our hay in London comes from Canada as this is too dusty for our horses,' which was a true statement as they would find out if they checked. I noticed a lot of chattering going on when she rejoined the others. So I began to realise farm work was very skilled or hard work or sometimes both together.

Mum bought me some second hand boots and trousers in Okehampton as my London boots were breaking up because of the wet and hard wear. They had to be second hand because my clothing ration coupons were needed to clothe the rest of the family their having lost everything. Anyway the boots came home wrapped in newspaper which I smoothed out to read. Apart from being dismayed at how the war was going I saw an advert by a firm called 'Friends of Wisbeach' who wanted mole-skins, paying one shilling to one shilling and sixpence in Summer time and two shillings to two shillings and sixpence in Winter.

So how to catch moles? I had seen mole traps but I would have to buy them and I still was not earning enough to splash out on something that, with my lack of skill, might be a waste of money. But there were so many mole-hills about! And in my minds eye I could see all this money running about. So I thought well moles ate worms and amongst the stuff of mine that was salvaged were little brass fish hooks, so I tied them on short bits of string with a peg on the other end and dug up a few worms, I did not tell Mum what I was doing - I knew it was daft, so I opened up some mole tunnels put the worms on a hook, dropped it in the tunnel, covered it and pushed the stick in the ground. I decided to wait 24 hours and the result was four lost hooks but two moles. When I went home I said, 'Look Mum - three shillings.' She looked at the advert said nothing, but the next week she brought home six brand new mole traps. She did not say how much they cost, but she told me the man at the ironmongers had said to bury them in the garden for a week to rid them of the smell of oil.

I was itching to start making a fortune, but country know-how told me to, so I buried them. There was some work going getting the corn harvest in, and I was earning most days. As we were leaving the field one evening another farmer said, 'I have a couple of days for you,' so I waited for the next bit, as the dung spreading joke was still circulating round, then he said, 'Horse riding,' I quickly told him I could not ride a horse, but he said all I had to do was sit on it and keep on flicking it with a stick, somebody else would be steering it. It seems this horse did not like anything that rattled behind it so would not go unless someone kept reminding it, but was okay ploughing, rolling or dragging, so that solved another country mystery as far as a London boy was concerned. There were adverts in the local papers saying 'horse for sale quiet in all gears.' Which I always thought was subtle country joke as it's so obvious horse has no gears! Whereas the gears of cars and lorries used to rattle in those days.

So two mornings later I set off 'to ride a horse'. I was not afraid of the horse as I'd had a close experience with one before. The farmer had said eight o'clock so I was there and so was the reaper but no-one else. A bit later on the farmer arrived and without even looking in my direction pulled the head off an ear of wheat, rubbed it in his hands and bit some, and walked off. Thinking that I was wasting my time here and it was getting on and there were other things I could be doing I headed for the gate just as the farmer came back and went through the same antics again. He turned to me and shouted 'Run back and tell the men to fetch the horses.' I went but they must have heard him because they were coming anyway.

The horses were harnessed up. The one I was to ride was on the offside, which meant if I were to fall off I would be in the way of the cutters, which resembled an eight foot long hedge trimmer with sharp toes and wicked looking blades which slashed backwards and forwards. The farmer said, 'Jump up boy.' Jump up? More like climbing a quivering lump with no handles or somewhere to put your feet. A hand grabbed my right leg and up I went. They gave me the switch. The driver was sitting about ten feet behind me and the last words to me was when he lays his ears back give him a flick, so off we went well with the clatter of the cutters and the switch of the sails that blow the corn over the knives and the rumbling noise of the endless belts carrying up to where it is tied into sheaves and the whack as it goes through the sheaf-out, the horses ears where laid back most of the time.

The farmer bellowed out 'stop' then he said I was to give the horse a flick dead centre over the root of its tail. Now to follow that instruction when I was sitting astride looking forward meant turning my upper body 90 degrees. Well I suppose a London boy should have known that so off we went again. I soon found out there were other things a London boy should have known, like taking my coat off as it was getting quiet hot and that I should have had a sack to sit on, because the chains and harness was making itself felt. After a seemingly interminable time we had come to a stop and the driver got down and said, 'Bate time boy.'

Somehow I got down and he unhooked the horses, took them into the shade of the hedge and put their nose bags on and walked off. I could not sit down so lent against the hedge and had a few cupped handfuls out of their bucket of water and ate my apple. I looked around the field, the sheaves were stood on their butt ends six at a time in straight lines across the field. My work had been half way between a horse's ears and its back-side and concentrated on not falling off. I had not noticed what the men were doing. When we were to start again I thought 'that could not possibly be an hour,' and the medieval torture started again. I did put my coat under me this time, but the damage had already been done.

After almost four and a half hours there was a brief stop; the little cutting knife had worked loose and as a result the shears could not leave the reaper and became jammed up. I did not get off. When the farmer called a halt, at the end of the day, he just said to me 'Eight tomorrow lad - half day.'

I walked home keeping my legs as wide apart as I could. Mum saw me coming and gave me some iodine and talcum powder. And I went in the barn and dabbed the iodine on the abrasions. My legs were raw down to the knee both sides - and a few other places. When I went in I said it would be a half day tomorrow. After a very uncomfortable night I did my usual jobs and was on the field by eight, but the corn was not ready until ten.

We stopped at twelve and I got down, the farmer came over the held out a hand-full of mixed coins. Now there are a lot of country jobs a London boy cannot do, but when it comes to a hand full of cash he can count, I quicker than anybody, and that handful was three hours short. I just stared at him. And his words were 'I hired you to ride the horse.' I still left the money in his hand. He finally gave in and fished the extra out of his waistcoat pocket and added it to the rest. I thought 'you have had your little game. So now I will have mine' so I took the money a few coins at the time and loudly and carefully added them up, by the time I had finished he was ready to explode. I thanked him and calmly walked away. I saw his farm hands sitting there taking in every detail.

I did ask a farm lad why I had to ride nearest the cutters. He said the one missing was the offside horse. Well surely they could be swapped over, I had suggested. He said the offside horse always follows the furrow. Well I suppose if you ask a silly question.

Chapter 22   of moles and cones

One morning with no job to go to I wandered out and in my wanderings I always carried a sack because you never know what you might find. I heard the sound of axes in a strip of pine trees on the high ground of Mr Penwarden's land. 'Might be the chance of a job.' I thought.

There were six men, two with axes cutting wedge shapes out of the base of the trees and four with chain saws. Something I had never heard of before. Well I did ask them if the chocks (wedges of wood cut before felling) were wanted. They jabbered away at one another. I realised they were foreign, that was good enough, so I started to pick up this ready cut fire wood. But one shook my arm and in mime showed me I was in the way of falling trees and pointed further along to where I would be safe and went and carried on filling my sack.

I became aware of a man in a decent suit coming my way. Before he could say anything I said, 'I'm only helping myself to these chocks, I did ask but they did not seem to understand.' 'They would not because they are Norwegian,' he said, 'It's alright about the wood, but why are you not working?' I told him I only did casual. He said, 'You can pick larch cones for me then.' I immediately looked up in the tree tops. He had a chuckle and said, 'No, after they have felled the trees. I'll show you.' and we went where they were already down and the tops were like big bushes. He showed me how only wanted the shiny ones to extract the seed to grow more. He would leave sacks for me to use and to put the cones on the lorry that collected the men at sunset. I was still waiting to hear the words that would make me say yes and he finally said, 'And what you have been waiting for is - six shillings a bushel.' I knew how much a bushel was because all the soft fruit from Kent came to Covent Garden in bushel baskets. So between other jobs I picked and put them on the lorry.

But nothing came at the weekend so what to do? Carry on picking or write it off as a loser? He had the cones and all I had was a few sackfuls of chocks. I decided to carry on and during the next week I began to run out of cones so on Thursday I put rest of the cones and the surplus sacks on the lorry. Friday, midday, the men packed up and the woods fell silent. And I'd had a lesson in human nature I really did not need.

In the following week I had a few jobs and I was catching eight or so moles so things were not too bad. Then, as I was passing Penwarden's Farmyard, someone called out and it was 'the suit' so I went in. He said that he had wondered why I had not sent any cones in for two days. I replied that my trust was a very delicate thing. He said, 'Oh dear then I hope I can restore it for you, according to my notes I owe you six pounds twelve and four pence,' and started to put the money in my hand. With that Mr Penwarden threw his hat on the ground and jumped on it and bellowed out, 'All that for picking cones? I'll give up farming and pick cones instead.' The suit said, 'Alas Mr Penwarden the lad has cleared them all and we have moved on,' and he shook my hand and wished me the best of luck. I went home with more than three weeks wages for a skilled man in my pocket.

I suggested to Mum we could invest in a few more mole traps. The work was drying up now the crops were in and my dozen mole traps were only catching eight or ten a week but the price they were paying had gone up, apparently the moles had now got their winter coats on. Seemed a bit queer to me but who was I to argue. I was out one day setting my traps and, true to say, I had not a clue whose land it was, I thought I was doing some farmer a favour as I had read in the local paper that moles in Devon alone were damaging thousands of acres of grass thus denying the farmers of the grazing. Anyway, I was busy cutting out the turf to put my traps down and I realised I was not alone.

The first hint was a pair of beautiful polished brown boots and as my eyes travelled upwards over legs clad in clean and pressed trousers, check shirt and waistcoat, bulging a bit at the top. And I suddenly realised it was a girl in trousers and when I had got over that initial shock I noticed her face. She was, what we called back then, a 'Mongol' (downs syndrome) girl. I'd seen downs girls before but they never seemed to live beyond ten years. She had some rabbit traps with her and a can with a wire handle. She had nice pigskin gloves on. I think I stuttered something like 'Am I in the wrong field?' She didn't answer but squatted down by me and shovelled some of the mole hill earth into her can. She was looking at me and her eyes were smiling but her mouth was snarling and she suddenly took my traps from my hand and standing up she looked around and started picking my traps and shaking her head. I thought, 'Oh no, I am going to lose my traps for being in the wrong place,' but then she stopped and pointed to two more of mine and I was thinking well that's the lot. But she was nodding and began setting my traps again in different places and I watched and realised I was getting a lesson in mole trapping and when she was finished I said thank you, and with a little flip of her hand she walked away. I then noticed she had a six inch sheath knife on her belt and I looked down at my traps and when I looked up again she had disappeared.

I went to the field next morning and I had ten moles so I reset the traps and as I was leaving there was the farmer and the first thing he said was, 'You won't get above two moles tomorrow.' Seeing my baffled expression he went on to say, 'Moles are solitary. There is only one in each system except in the breeding season. Oh - and I have two more fields over by the river you can trap them.' I said I had met the young lady and that I hadn't seen her before, 'You wouldn't,' he said, 'but she has seen you - as we all have. You're a good lad so nobody minds where you wander.' And then he laughed and said, 'but I shan't hire you to ride a horse; you're too expensive,' and went away chuckling.

When I told Mum that the farmer seemed amused at what I do, she understood and said I had to remember that their horizons were small. That apart from the business of running their farms and making enough to pay the rent and occasional visits to Okehampton for the stock market with their wives to buy whatever they could not make or grow, that was their whole life. Indeed, as I gradually found out, very few had been to Exeter, twenty-one miles away, and even fewer had been to the coast.

Only the Squire and the Vicar had cars so it seemed we were a welcome diversion.

I got some work picking apples and also lifting mangelwurzels, that was literally pulling them out of the ground chopping the tops off and throwing them up in the cart. Quite a few weighed seven kilos and the side of the cart was eight foot high. That certainly built my muscles.

One evening at the chapel I asked a farmer if I could catch his moles. He said, 'Yes lad but you will have to wait until I get some more – you've already trapped the ones I had,' and the chapel exploded with laughter. I told Mum 'I think I just gave them something else to brighten their lives.' The furriers must have thought I was a good supplier for with the next remittance they put a printed card naming what they needed. And it included badger, fox, rabbit, mole, stoat, weasel, jay wings. And down the other edge were boxes where you entered the number of each in the consignment. I never saw the girl again but sometimes a trap would be in a different place which invariably had a mole in it.

As the evenings were drawing in Mum also started us on other projects indoors. We picked a lot of the apples in the orchard and cored them, sliced them, threaded on willow rods and put them over the stove to dry so Mum could make apple crumble in the winter. Mum was getting old woollen jerseys from somewhere, they were washed, unravelled, and she taught us how to crochet. So Mum, Aunt Bess, me and Peter were turning out twenty centimetre squares which were sewn together to make much needed blankets.

We were now well into December. Mum had me find a bit of a bush with a lot of twigs and when Peter and Dorothy were in bed, we wound coloured paper round the twigs to make a Christmas tree and decorated it with glass baubles that came from home in London and small novelties that Mum had bought in Okehampton. On Christmas Eve I brought in some nicely berried holly and we decorated the beams. Mum had got a nice duck for Christmas dinner. I walked into South Tawton with a medicine bottle and the manager of the Seven Stars pub filled it with port for me for one shilling and six pence so we could give Aunt Bess a present and a nice surprise. We had a nice Christmas, sung a few carols and wondered how Dad was getting on.

Chapter 23   Devon snow

New Year 1941 arrived and one morning soon after, when I woke, there was a funny sort of light at the window and when I looked out it had snowed so I called Peter. We thought it was so deep it had buried the garden wall and it was piled up the front of the cottage. So I went down and it *was covering the windows*! I got the fire going and Mum came down and opened the front door to a solid wall of snow!

Mum said that after a bit of breakfast we will have to dig our way out and as the back door opened outwards that way would be impossible. The only shovel we had indoors was a small fire shovel - the big shovel was out in the barn. So Peter and I started to tunnel our way out. Having got out we realised the garden wall must have collapsed in the night and was now covered by the snow. I got into the barn and retrieved the big shovel and started to dig, but I was not getting on too well because the snow was sticking to the shovel. Mum was watching from upstairs. She called out 'Pass it up to me,' and in about five minutes she handed it out again clean and shining. She had warmed it up and rubbed candle wax on it and now the snow didn't stick. How many Mums would have thought of that? But as her Mother was Cornish perhaps it was 'inherited' memory.

I cleared the snow away from the downstairs windows and round the pump, primed it and filled the buckets. A farmer arrived with his worker and gave Mum a chunk of pork and a few pounds of potatoes to tide us over until the thaw, and asked if I would I go with them to find and dig out sheep buried in the drifts. 'He'll be a while Mrs,' he said, 'we don't know quite where they be. Tuck your trousers into your socks lad,' he said, 'and bring the shovel,' but when he saw it he said, 'That's no good lad - never mind we'll pick up one at the farm,' and so we did. It was heart-shaped on a 2 metre pole that I could just get my hand around! (remember, I was still only fourteen) They cut me a long thin hazel rod with one sharp end to probe with and off we went.

I was already soaked to the knees, but after struggling in drifts up to my waist and probing to a point where I thought that perhaps he didn't have any sheep and this was of their 'London boy' jokes, I was soaked through to the waist and I could not feel my feet at all. Then one of the others found a sheep, and it was 'Now prod gently boy,' though my hands did not know whether they were holding a stick or not - but I found one. Then it was 'scrape the snow away carefully' ... and gradually I found its back and when I got to it, the ungrateful beast, exploded from the snow, knocked me backwards into the drift and used me as a running board to get out. Well, at around forty kilos on four sharp hoofs, it left a few dents in me.

We got the lot out. I did ask whether they would have frozen, and the answer was no, but they would starve. Seeing my puzzled expression he then said, 'But if they were close to one another they would chew the fleece of one another and then die of rumen compaction.' I believed it as it sounded too complicated for a London boy joke. We drove them back to the farm and I struggled along, they did ask if I was all right I said yes; I could not admit I thought

I was dying of frost bite like those arctic explorers. After all London boys were tougher than that weren't they? As I hobbled home and circulation started to come back I could not tell if my feet were on fire or I was walking on broken glass. Just think - in those days there were no waterproof trousers or gloves and Wellingtons were in short supply.

When I got in Mum had the kitchen really warm and had sent the others off to bed early. She had hot soup on the stove, gave me a blanket, warned me not to get warm too quickly and went to bed. It amazed me how Mum seemed to know in advance what I would need when I was in trouble. When I stripped my clothes off I was blue up to my rib cage, and my appendages seem to have disappeared; bothered me - that did - I could not help wondering if it would be permanent. I hung my clothes over the stove and stretched out on some chairs and as I became gradually warm I dozed off.

I awoke to the smell of cocoa, sometime in the night Mum had come down and put an old overcoat over me, and now she had porridge on the go. She gave me my clothes and went upstairs again so I dressed, glad to see everything was back as it ought to be. My clothes were so dry they were stiff and crackled like paper.

I did ask an old chap why the others did not seem to get wet and the reply was 'That be the lanolin.' I thought - well ask a silly question. I began to realised how tough farm people were and skilled at what they do, and their care of animals beyond anything townspeople would comprehend.

The snow began to melt and Mr Penwarden came up to the cottage to tell us that icicles would form on the edge of the thatch and not to knock them off because they would tear the thatch away, but to leave them and if the thaw continued they would detach themselves. That was when we found out what the corrugated iron porch was for. If one of those icicles was to hit you when you went out the door ... I will leave you to imagine.

Chapter 24   to be a farmer's boy

Eventually the snow cleared and soon after Mum had been told that a farmer wanted a lad and that was it - if a job was available during the wartime you had to take it. Seven shilling and six pence cash - a considerable drop to what I had been making - but the law is the law and he was expecting me next morning. It was around six miles away and I arrived at seven in the morning, he was standing in the yard and his greeting was 'There you are - I've been waiting.' My instinct was turn around and go but I was trapped. He said, 'Come on I will show you where you will sleep. Then we will have to get on with the milking.' In a flash I thought 'a get-out!' so I said, 'I can't milk,' and then the trap closed again. He said, 'No, but you can soon learn - so get moving, the churn has to be at the top of the lane by eight.'

We went into the shippen which is the name for a cow house. To my surprise it was warm in there. He lit a couple of storm lanterns and I could then see the rear ends of eight cows with dungy sides - caused by when they lie down in what they deposit during the night. He sat me down on a three legged stool, showed me how to grip the bucket between my calves with the rim at the bottom nestling on my ankles to keep the bottom out of the dung and to keep your balance you put the top of your head against the cow's side, then he said, 'Moisten your hands with a drop of milk, grip the teats with the thumb and forefinger now squeeze the milk out with the other fingers,' and so I started. First off, when you put your milky hands on the teat after a few squeezes there were brown drips coming off your hands and going in the bucket, but I gradually got the hang of it. And then found another snag. Cow's were not immobile and would move suddenly in any direction which threatened to tip you off the stool or they would flick their tails and the dungy end would slap you round the back of the neck. When he said, 'Haven't you finished that one yet?' I didn't answer, but thought 'sack me mister please.' But no luck.

I found out much later he was as much stuck with me as I was with him. Me, because of reasons already stated and him, because none in the farming community would work for him. The young horseman he had he got by buying the smallholding the man lived in as a tied cottage, which meant he had to work for the farmer or lose his home. That's when I began to understand the strained atmosphere. Orders given; just a nod for reply, no good mornings not even comments about the weather. He would talk to me, but only briefly, if the farmer was not around.

Well the milking got finished, my two, to his six, and we carried the buckets to the back of the house and he showed me how to strain it, that meant pouring it through a cloth that smelt of cheese, into the churn which was the old tall variety, which was then trundled across the cobbled yard and onto the trolley which was made from an old side-car chassis which was then dragged up the lane to a stand, which was as high as the bed of a lorry. Well the churn top was chest high to me and the handles half way up so when I bent and grabbed the handles and stood up the bottom of the churn was only half as high as it needed to go. I did get it there eventually thinking 'not only were London boys good for nothing but they are not even tall enough - or strong enough.'

I went back to the house and I was asked if I had got it there in time. I did not know when they took the full churn they left an empty one. It seemed to me if there was not a full one to pick up they would not have left an empty one, so how would I know, so I said nothing. He muttered something and indicated where I should sit on a form behind a table that was big enough for at least ten.

His wife, who was cooking breakfast, had not said a word and was frying something over the fire. He growled 'We have a days work to do,' so she plated it and I got mine. It was a fair heap of chopped up pork belly and boiled potatoes, also chopped, and the lot fried in pork fat. Well I came from a time when you ate what you could get so undeterred I waded in - and then there was dough cake, which was the soft bread yellowed with saffron that you put home made jam on. I thought if I get this three times a day I won't mind, and then he said, 'Now you're finally finished take your bag up those stairs to your bed and come straight down. There's work to do!'

This turned out to be digging all the dungy straw from round the cows' legs and throwing it on the dung hill outside and bedding the cows on clean straw - which they immediately soiled. Followed by filling the hay racks, putting mangelwurzels through the chopper and giving a bucketful to each cow. The chopper was powered by a big handle which you turned by hand or, in my case, my full weight, and decreasing energy. Next, it transpired, we were 'dagging' sheep before lunch. I thought here we go again with the funny talk, then he said get the shears from the linney and a bucket. The linney turned out to be a shed. I thought 'I know what shears are' - even in London they were used to trim privet hedges, but I could not see any and then he came in shouting 'What are you poking around in here for?' snatched something and threw it in the bucket.

I knew this man was on a very short fuse but, as we trudged out to the field I thought, 'if he does not stop using dialect on me I will start using rhyming slang.' Anyway, when we had got the sheep penned up he showed me how to turn one upside down; simple enough, you leant over the sheep, grabbed the wool as low as you could down the other side and by pulling upwards roll the sheep up your legs until it is in the right position. *Easy enough if you are strong enough - and at least as heavy as the sheep!* Then you hold the sheep with one hand and with the shears you trim away all the dungy wool from their tail and backside. Otherwise flies will lay eggs in it when the weather warms, also so it's clear when the lambs arrive in about another month. Then I had to pick up all the dungy wool to go under his runner beans. I was getting the idea that nothing was wasted. By the time we were finished I understood about the lanolin - the front of my trousers was shiny and slippery with it.

Then it was back for lunch which, I have to say, smelt beautiful. A big bowl of thick stew chopped up fat pork again, spuds and onion and the spoon really stood up in it. After dinner he said, 'Get your overcoat there will be a cold wind up on the hill.' Mum had got me an army surplus great-coat dyed dark green. He muttered to his wife 'I will be up at the clamp for three sacks of spuds.' Well I thought I knew what a clamp was and it had nothing to do with spuds. Off we went with two of those useless long handled shovels. When we got there he was right about the wind. He started scraping earth down the side of a long earth ridge with straw sticking out of the top. So I started on the other side. He said when you get to the straw remove it carefully and keep it straight - and there were the spuds. We knelt on an old sack and sorted out the best and unblemished ones went into the sacks, for whatever purpose he never said, and the rest into the bucket. Despite my overcoat I was feeling cold for the wind was hitting me before him. He then told me to push the two shovels into the ground about a metre apart and drape my great-coat over them. I thought 'here we go, I take my coat off and he keeps his on, but he will only pull this stroke once,' however I was really surprised when I knelt down again to find it warmer. Eventually the sacks were filled, the clamp resealed, and we went back to the farm carrying the bucket of imperfect spuds which Mrs had to use in the kitchen. I don't know what happened to the sacks of spuds they were never mentioned again, I suppose they were sold.

I was taken out to the stable and shown a Clydesdale mare which I would have to harness and put between the shafts of whatever piece of equipment he said. I was shown the harness. The first piece he gave me was the saddle which I knew about having had painful contact with one once before. I was to get it on the back of this frightening mass of horse about six feet high (two metres). 'You throw the girth over first,' he said. I could not hold the saddle up against her side let alone throw the girth, but by balancing it on my head with my left hand and then standing on the tips of my toes I got it there. 'Now reach under and get hold of the girth,' that was easy enough if I ducked down under this great belly, so I buckled it up my side and then the next instruction was 'pull it up tight' and when I did he suddenly said, 'Damn you Bess' and her stomach shrank and I was able to reach more holes on the buckle. It seems she was having her own game with this idiot.

In a note aside here, I will say that in the course of time Bess and I came to understand one another, especially when I started to give her a few oats in the palm of my hand. Her normal grooming and feeding was down to the horseman and was strictly administered. The horseman said one morning 'Keep your hands out of the oat chest.' I said, 'It was only a few for when she let me put the harness on.' He shook his head and said, 'You think she is letting you harness her for a few oats but she will start to play up again and you will increase the oats and so on it will go until one day she will collapse, poisoned by too much oats for the work she's done on a daily basis, which I regulate.' I said I was sorry and thanks for the lesson and then asked is it the same as colic? Now he asked 'What do you know about colic?' and I told him about the one that fell against my legs and they cut its throat. He looked incredulous and I said, 'This happened in London?' and then he asked, 'How many horses in London?' I said, 'They are everywhere. There are over a hundred horses in the

Great Western Railway stables not a hundred yards from where I lived.' He still looked doubtful but said, 'Someone must have let it drink too fast' and then he said as he walked away, 'If she plays up again just rub your fingers through the oats and then just put your hand over her muzzle as you talk to her by name and the soft talk will take the place of the oats.' I thought I had just received a pearl that was not given lightly. I did try to say thanks but he was on his way with the other pair of horses. And that was the most I ever heard him say at once in the rest of the time I was there.

The rest of that first day was spent showing me things and then it was milking time again and after that feeding the weaned calves - that was a game on its own. They had a half and half mix of milk and warm water in a bucket and they were not allowed to drink it on their own as apparently they would suck in air and inflate their stomachs. So you had to grip their nose put two fingers in their mouth then dip their noses in the bucket and then they sucked the milk past your fingers. Me, I just wondered if there was anything animals could do on their own. Anyway that first evening after a bit of supper Mr and Mrs disappeared – no good night or anything said.

I went up to my room and really looked at it for the first time. It was immediately over the kitchen, rough floor boards and no ceiling, just the underside of the roof and one small window the same as the kitchen. I suppose it was meant to keep warm by the heat rising from the kitchen. The bed itself was colder than the room so I decided to keep my socks on in bed and I soon found I needed my overcoat laid on the bed as well. As I had not been offered any washing facilities I went down, got myself some hot water in a bucket from the big kettle that hung over the fire, and had a wash in that.

Chapter 25   calves and lambs

When I went home on my Wednesday afternoon off I asked Mum for a flannel and towel and soap as I needed a full body wash down and change of clothes on my day off and so a routine was started.

The Farmer and his wife had a small daughter, I hadn't seen her walking but she used to be in a small rocking chair in the kitchen. Sometimes she scared me the way she got the chair rocking and would then throw her head backwards as the back was coming forward, resulting in several hard knocks to the back of the head.

On the way back to the farm one bitterly cold and drizzly night I thought I would cut about two hundred meters off the walk by crossing the home meadow heading for the kitchen window light. So I got over the gate and keeping my eyes on the light. I walked and over half way there I suddenly tripped and fell across the back of a sheep laid there. Well, what with me falling down and her exploding up in fright all that soaking wet wool hit me in the face and I rolled in the wet grass and when I got to my knees I could not see the light. When I stood up again, there it was, and I realised that when you were close to the ground your horizon was shortened. And so was my journey but I was soaking wet - not a very good swap.

Another cow calved and about one more gallon went in the churn. When I tried to lift it on the stand by the road I had to go back to the two lifts. I knew the weight of water per cubic foot, it's all part of physics at school but you never equated it with milk. One day when I was in the yard a cattle lorry arrived and unloaded a cow and calf and Mr led the cow over with the calf following as quiet as you like and he opened the root-store house door, one side of which was like a stable door with two halves, and the other side was a plain door, both closing onto a centre post. When she was quietly inside he called me to hold onto the bridle, when he was sure I had hold - I twisted the rope around my wrist to make sure I could not drop it - he picked up the calf and walked out, apparently to be take it away. The calf cried out like it was being killed and the cow went berserk and tried to get over the stable door, which was open a fraction, and I knew I could not hold her so I pulled the rope around the centre post which immediately became detached top and bottom. So a mad cow, a ten foot post plus an idiot London boy went charging across the yard. The men got the lorry doors shut and jumped in the cab. Mr had disappeared and the calf had gone quiet, Mr reappeared and said, 'Damn you boy you could have got somebody injured - don't you know anything?' I didn't know that the post was *supposed* to be removable.

At breakfast one morning he said, 'I want you to walk about the sheep, the lambing is due to start., I asked 'Is that before or after milking?' (As my milking had improved Mr had stopped helping me) 'After' was the reply and that he would look at five o'clock. I was still getting up at six to complete the milking, I was getting better at it but when another cow calved there was the extra milk, but I was managing, so I thought, but now by the time I had taken the churn up to the road and walked amongst the sheep, the calves were bellowing for their feed. And by the time I satisfied them Mr was shouting me for breakfast.

When I got in my pork and spuds had gone cold and congealed I still scoffed it but you would have thought the lady would have put it on the stove. Several lambs were born that day, I also realised where baby's came from and that you had to move the slimy limp object so the ewe could lick it, I tried to rub the slime off with a piece of sack but was told that her licking would get it breathing best but that, if it would not breathe, to pick it up by its back legs and swing it vigorously back and forth. I didn't look at his face to see if this was another joke to tell down the chapel but suddenly the lamb spluttered and bleated and he said, 'Well, that's another live one.' Then he said, 'You come out a check all's well at ten o'clock and I'll check at 12 and you can do it at 4 in the morning, seeing as you are already getting out at six to milk.'

The lambing took place out in an open field in the bitter cold and sometimes rain, not in big sheds with lights and deep dry straw as you see on the telly nowadays, it's a wonder the lambs were born at all. He made up a bottle of whisky and water that stood by the stove that I was to take with me when I went out to check at night, I thought 'What, some consideration shown at last?' so when I went out at four I had a good swig and felt much better about life in general. At four I found two had been born and moved them to the hedge, out of the wind, and another was on its way two little hooves were showing and the tip of its nose. So I thought I better wait for it and had another swig and out it came, I put it under the hedge and the ewe started to do her bit. I went in and it had gone five. Useless to go to bed I know so I started milking a bit early so the churn was up the road early and the calves were fed early.

About half seven he came out realised I was all done and then he blew his top. It was 'Damn boy there will be less milk in the churn!' I said, 'Well it will be made up by tonight.' He roared 'No it won't, an udder only holds what it holds there is no room for the extra so what you did not get this morning will be lost forever, much more of your stupidity and I will be bankrupt!' When we went in to breakfast he did not say another word about what had transpired, but while we were eating he kept turning and looking over at the stove and his wife thinking there was something she had done wrong I suppose, said, 'What's wrong dear?' and without looking at me said, 'How many new lambs did you see this morning?' I said, 'Three.' He said, 'Did they get on their feet?' I said, 'No,' and he shouted, 'No wonder, they must be blind drunk!' The word 'whoops' went through my mind.

The next few days went along the same way - the only bright spot was when I was tacking up Bess one morning I was soft talking and as I brushed my hand down her back, where I saw hog seed had fallen from the hay loft above, her back sagged down, it must have been by at least fifteen centimetres, so I put the saddle on and she immediately straightened up again. That was marvellous. And the horseman said,

'She's yours boy.' I really felt great about that, and the lambing seemed to be going well too.

Then one morning, after I'd been lambing all night, the Farmer came into breakfast and said, 'There's a ewe down with two lambs off but she has another to come,' he said, 'leave that,' pointing at my breakfast, 'there's another lamb to get off.' When we got to the ewe he said, 'This is where you start learning to be a shepherd, now kneel down there put your hand in and find out what's wrong.' It's a good job I had not had my breakfast 'he must be mad' I thought but I did try and was amazed how easy it was. Then he said, 'Can you feel the head?' 'No, but there are two legs.' Then he asked 'Are they front or back?' I looked up at him and before I could ask how would I know he said, 'Hurry up, can you feel the tail,' I nodded. He said, 'Take hold of the hooves and when she strains draw the lamb out,' I said, 'I felt the hooves.' And he exploded 'Why did you not say so before?' I thought to reply - but I suppose a London boy ought to know everything. He went on 'Now when she is not heaving push the rump forward and bring the legs back.' After a couple of attempts, I got them and I started to draw it out. The next instruction was 'Use your other hand and keep the chest compressed until the head is clear - clean its mouth out and let go the chest - now swing it!' It spluttered shook its head and cried out - the ewe got up and, before I could get to my feet, butted me over. His words of praise to me were 'That should have been done before - you're lucky it is still alive.'

After all that it was a very little lamb. I was thinking that was one bit of farming I did not want to repeat but, funnily enough, that particular piece of skill was to be of use to me much later in life. Before the end of the lambing I got two more, one the ewe was exhausted and had stopped pushing, that was easy, the other one had its umbilical round its neck, I realised what I had to do and after a bit of pushing and shoving got it off and gave myself a congratulatory swig. Before the end of lambing he showed me how to take the skin off a dead lamb and fit it on an orphan so the mother would accept it as her own.

I looked round for the little lamb later and asked where it was. He said, 'In the oven.' I thought 'I won't ask' but when I went in for breakfast the lamb was in the warming oven, keeping warm, and my breakfast was on top. I did help get a calf of sometime later but that involved ropes.

Chapter 26   rams, stallions and slag

One day at teatime he said, 'At eight tonight a cattle wagon will arrive at Belstone Cross, be there, I am having a ram delivered - take a piece of binder twine with you and bring it back.' I was there, the wagon arrived, the driver and his mate had a struggle to get it out. I said, 'He said a ram not a pony!' 'It's a Southdown,' they said. I had seen smaller ponies on stage at the Queens theatre. Perhaps I should have made a bridle out of the twine but I just tied it round its neck. I do not think it was ever led anywhere before because it just went mad and took off, luckily for me in the right direction.

The road went down hill, I attempted to make it ease up because I could hardly keep my feet so when I jerked on the twine it turned sharp left and went up the hedge and when I pulled it down it knocked me flat. This sort of behaviour carried on until I got it in the field with the ewes. I went in and the clock now said twenty to ten, all that time for less than a mile - there was no sign of Mr and Mrs so I bathed my grazes and bruises and went to bed.

At breakfast he said, 'That ram's alright?' I nodded he said, to nobody in particular, 'I don't know whether he's deaf, dumb or daft'. And Mrs said, 'Why did you want another ram Dear?' I think to ease the tension. He answered quite calmly 'It's a Southdown. With him the ewes will throw bigger lambs so I can get a better price and feed all the extra mouths around here.' She went a funny colour, and left the table. He turned and looked at me. But I was thinking of the ewes were having trouble lambing now what will it be like with bigger lambs but I did not ask.

He said, 'Come on, I have never known a boy to dawdle over a meal like you, let's see the ram.' As soon as he put his hand on the gate I saw the ram put its head down to charge but Mr had just got through the gate when he saw it coming and tried to come out. But 'Damn boy' had put the latch on and the ram smashed into the back of his legs. He hollered and slashed back at it with his stick. It reared up on its hind legs to do the typical downward butt, and have never seen such a big man climb over a gate so fast, and when the ram struck he broke one of the gate 'shettals' (dialect for the thin narrow planks across the gate width). By the time he turned to look at me I was gazing into the trees with my mouth hanging open, thinking my own thoughts. I did realise that the ram stayed well away from the dog which, though an elderly sheep dog, I made sure to take with me when I went to check on the sheep.

One morning he gave me a big penknife, the blade was hooked at the point, and said, 'Take it to the stone and put a good edge on it. We are docking lambs after breakfast.' I sharpened it pondering on the docking as the only docking I knew involved large ships and lock gates but with the dagging in mind I kept quiet and soon found out. One of you picked up the lamb and the other one cut its tail off. He did two, I did the rest, and the male lambs were castrated at the same time using a big pair of chrome-plated pinchers. We gathered up all the lambs' tails for Mrs to skin and make a lambs-tail pie with. By that time any change from pork was welcome and it did not taste too bad either.

One day it was 'clear out the garage'. So I did that, useless to ask why, and next day a dapper little man arrived dressed in immaculate jodhpurs, yellow waistcoat, cravat and a beautiful hacking jacket and the shiniest pair of boots and gaiters I had ever seen, and he was leading the biggest shire horse I had ever seen too. The farmer was there to meet him and I understood a deal had been done whereby the stallion would be stabled in the garage for two nights, while the stallion visited all the mares that farmers had booked him for and, in exchange for the stabling, my boss would get two matings on Bess and she would be first on this local tour.

I heard the farmer telling the groom that he did not know Bess' history. I understood later that if a mare has not had a foal before she is nine years old she never would. They took the stallion through a field gate and sent me to lead out Bess. The farmer took hold of the bridle and led her to the gate with him one side and her the other. That puzzled me I'd taken cows down to the bull and knew that at least they had to be both on the same side. So I was not prepared for what happened next. The stallion reached over the gate and sniffed at her mane, she whirled round so fast and kicked out with her back legs and the stallion reared backwards. The farmer gave me the halter and said run her back to her stable quick! Apparently the stallion can't be calmed down until the mare is out of sight. Now I understood the gate, if it had not been there she would have ruined thousands of pounds worth of horse.

In the building adjoining the stables there were six pigs that Mr fed, and one morning I heard him throw the door open and it hit the wall with a bang and the pigs broke through under Bess's manger just as I began putting her harness on. She reared up as the squealing pigs went through her legs. I hung on her halter and as I got her legs down she let fly with her back legs and her hooves struck sparks from the wall, the pigs passed behind the other horses and they lashed out too, the pigs went out the door. He started shouting for me to head the pigs off but I never heard, struck as I was by the intermittent deafness, with which I was becoming afflicted. He came back in the stable and shouted 'I was calling you boy!' 'Oh were you?' I said, 'I was calming your horse and checking she had not loosened her shoes.' 'If she has - that will be another expense!' he snapped. All I could think was if he had not banged the sty door open in temper I would not have had ten seconds of a ton of horse plunging and letting fly with her dinner-plate-sized hooves in a narrow stall. And not so much as 'are you all right boy?' from him either.

At another time he had us help him catch the pigs up, by now quite sturdy young pigs. He and the horseman were to catch a pig and I had to hold the sack open ready for them to put it in, and even then it was a struggle. After the first was in and tied I noticed how the pigs were running round and round the edge of the sty, avoiding being caught, so instead of just holding the sack ready I held it open down against the wall and, as a pig ran into it, I snatched it up. (rather like catching a mouse back in London)

At that moment they caught one of the other pigs and turned to me for the open sack. Mr assumed I hadn't tied and put the previous sack down and began to shout – but I said, 'I have another pig in here,' then he saw the other sack already tied up. Soon all four pigs were in their sacks and he put them in the back of the cart and drove off with them.

One Friday he said, 'I haven't the chance to pay you today as I have not the change would it be all right if I pay you once a fortnight?' I said OK as I knew Mum was making money, but thought if you think I won't be counting you're deluding yourself.

One morning he declared he had some labour coming to help harvest the spuds and to go and collect up a few buckets. Two women arrived and soon he was ploughing out spuds and we were picking them up. The best were put in a pile but the small and the over large ones, which were cut in pieces each piece having eyes, were taken to the other side of the field and put in new furrows, about thirty centimetres apart, and ploughed in. I was confused – I thought you planted in the spring. By late afternoon we were finished, about one third of the goods were loaded on the butt cart and taken to where the previous clamp had been, of which there was now no sign, and clamped up. The rest were taken to the farmyard, bagged and weighed up and a day or two later a lorry came and took them away.

When I next saw Mr Penwarden I asked him what it was all about, he laughed, looked all around even though we were at least half a mile from the nearest person, and said the Ministry of Agriculture Executive decrees that every farmer, according to their total acreage, plant a percentage to spuds, even if their land was totally unsuitable, so there was little profit in it, so they played their own game. Later on a man did arrive, measured the area planted, filled in his forms to say the order had been complied with.

The dirtiest job I think, at least it was for me, was spreading basic slag on grassland. Slag was the dross raked off the top of the crucibles in the big foundries that was then ground up so it was literally iron dust which, when spread on grassland, enriched the grass and made it dark. Mr drove the cart, I stood in the back shovelling the slag and casting it in a wide arc. Now imagine standing in an unsteady cart and the shovel-full weighs seven kilos and, as you swing it, the weight decreases rapidly leaving you unsteady but you have to get the next one on its way and so on.

When we reached the other side of the field I realised why he was wearing an old mac with the collar turned up and a hat on. He could have warned me, I would have tied a piece of rag round my face, there being no masks or goggles back then, but I had no chance to prepare. Without stopping he turned the cart and carried on parallel to the last run, but now I was throwing the slag into the wind - and he did not stop until the field was covered. At least that was what he hoped because he said, 'I hope you have covered it all boy because if you have not when the grass darkens you will be able to see the light patches from the main road and they (other farmers) will comment on it.'

I thought 'Oh well Mum said they had small lives,' I was more concerned about the state I was in.

Amongst other things, I now knew what iron tasted like and it would be another three days before I could change my clothes but I was not going to show a weakness and ask if I could go home for an hour or two and give him the pleasure of saying no. How different things would have been if he had only talked and explained things. I felt he was incapable and as I learnt, at a later date, the family had always had borstal boys before the war and as I was informed they were used as punch bags by him and his brothers and because those boys could not retaliate or protest - that was bullying of the worst kind.

I took some of my mole traps there and began catching anything from six to ten a week and I cleared two meadows of moles. So one morning when he said, 'You're trapping moles.' I thought, like other farmers, he would be pleased. Instead he said, 'How many are you getting?' so I told him and he slammed the newspaper down on the table then, latching on to the biggest number, shouted 'You have been getting a pound a week and they look like my traps!' I said, 'I have a receipt at home.' Then he said, 'I never gave you permission. In future I want at least fifteen shilling of that.' I agreed but took my traps home. I might be an ignorant London boy but I was not going to start paying for my own bed, food and wages. He could catch his own moles.

The stallion came back and this time Bess liked the idea so I was told to lift her offside hoof up onto my knees so that when the stallion mounts she won't change her mind and kick - with one hoof off the ground she couldn't, and keep my head down so I would not get his hoof in my head. Now why not explain all that before? So I did as I was told, she let me lift her hoof and just as I was getting settled and thinking I was now holding up a quarter of Bess, when the stallion mounted. I felt the sudden extra weight and the great hoof close to the back of my neck. Just as I thought we were all going to topple over they shouted 'Keep her hoof up until they get the stallion away.' And then 'Get her back to the stable, boy.' Just as I was thinking that I was never going to stand upright again.

One day he said, 'There will be two churns up top soon'. I wondered why but did not bother to ask why. All the calves had been born and the shippen was full but the next thing I knew an in-calf Friesian arrived. At that time there were not too many about. I understood they were not too popular because of the very low butter fat that went with the high milk yield. (In these modern times the butter fat in Friesians and Holsteins is raised by feeding them a light protein diet). So one morning I looked in the loose box and she had calved. I did not know what she had been in calf by, but the calf was two thirds the size of a Devon calf and as I opened the top half of the door the calf leapt straight up in the manger I shut the door and went to do the milking.

I was busy when he came out and opened both top and bottom doors and went in and the calf came straight out. I had never seen a calf go so fast, Mr came out shouting for me - I went deaf again - after all I had to catch the milk lorry, they had only to catch the calf. However, they did not as it seemed to have disappeared by the time they got back. I finished the milking and had taken about six gallons off the Friesian. He was about to bellow at me but I said, 'Milk lorry.' That stopped him. He then told me to share the Friesian milk between the two churns and top them up with the other cows milk. He did help me drag the, now overloaded trolley, up the lane and when we went for breakfast, he said to no-one in particular, 'I put sixteen gallons in the churns this morning,' and there was I thinking that I did it. But Mrs said, 'That's good dear.'

About two weeks later at breakfast his milk cheque arrived and he looked around the table almost smiling and opened the envelope stared at it, growled, read the accompanying invoice, threw it down on the table, banged his fist down on it and he went out. I had a look at the invoice, and it said in effect that the milk marketing board had rejected the milk from the last three days of the month there being seriously below the required butter fat content and they sincerely hoped this problem will soon be solved.

When I went out he was just standing there. I waited for him to say something but he did not so I carried on with my routine jobs. Thinking 'wait until he gets his next months cheque' he will be discounted at least another seven days and, unless he tells me something different, I will carry on the way he instructed. At dinnertime he said, 'Use the Friesian's milk for the calves.' The Friesian was disposed of and I never knew what happened to the calf.

Bess never came on heat again, so was presumed pregnant.

Chapter 27   threshers and shearers

When I went home for my half day off, Mum showed me a letter that said Dad was sending down a bicycle that had been my Uncle Tom's and was practically new. He could no longer ride it because his right arm was badly wounded while taking part in an attack on German positions on Catania plain in Sicily and was now practically useless. In the envelopes was a ticket to be presented to the station master at Okehampton station. Next morning, at breakfast, I showed the ticket to Mr and asked if he would run me to the station in his car, expecting him to say 'no', in which case I intended to walk there after tea. But he agreed, and said we would go after dinner, and after dinner of we went. I gave the station master the ticket. He unlocked a door and wheeled the bike out. It was beautiful – all chrome and bright – just like new. Mr was standing behind me and he said to the station master 'That cannot possibly be the one.' but the station master said, 'I can assure you it is.' I thanked the man and wheeled it outside.

Mr, in an angry tone, said, 'Why would your uncle give you a bike like that?' So I replied in a similar tone 'Because he could no longer ride it anymore because he lost his arm fighting for King and Country which, incidentally, he does not own a square inch of.' By look at his face I could not work out if he was jealous or what, but we were attracting a few onlookers, so I decided to give him a bit more so I carried on saying. 'He would not have taken money from me even if I was earning enough to pay because I am family.' He said, 'But that's worth ...'

but before he could say how much I said, 'To me – yes, to him – no,' whereupon he suddenly realized we had an audience, flung himself in the car and roared off. I enjoyed my steady ride back to the farm. I put my bike in the cart shed and he was quickly there shouting 'You have got time to make up boy, from today the cows are laying out.' That would mean less mucking out but I would have to get up even earlier to fetch them from the field and return them and still beat the milk lorry before breakfast.

'So that's no hardship' I thought, but a few mornings later I woke up to a rattling noise, jumped out of bed. It was the horseman throwing pebbles at my window, by the time I got down and outside he had got the cows in for me. By the time I took the churns up the lane the lorry arrived. I thanked the horseman for his help, and as he turned away he said, 'Master was looking at that nice bike of yours.' I gave him a nod and took the front wheel out and took it to my room. The horseman in a subtle way was a friend. He never talked about anything but said the odd word or two which was encouraging or cautioning.

One morning as I was bowling a full churn across the cobbled yard the top slipped out of my hands and the churn fell on its side. The milk slapped the inside of the lid and it came off. I snatched the churn upright, added some water and put the lid back on. Well anybody who has spilt milk knows a cupful looks like a pint and a pint looks like a gallon. I won't say what a gallon looks like on a cobbled yard. I put the churn on the trolley and then ran around like a scalded cat with buckets of water washing it along the gully until I washed it out of the farmyard and then did a record trip up to the road with the churns.

Later that day the horseman said, 'The duck pond was a funny colour this morning. I walked the horses through it to stir the mud up. I had to take the horses to the stream because the horse trough was empty.' That's the way he was. He knew instantly what had happened and covered it up for me but with a rebuke because the trough was empty. It was spring fed, but slowly, so I topped it up before Mr saw it.

As time dragged by the constant routine was getting to me, I was not meeting anybody my own age and apart from reading my own history books there was nothing to do. There were no newspapers and no radio.

A week or so later I had heard a lot of steam engine noise from somewhere. I recognised that from tugs on the Thames and steam wagons on the London roads. About mid-morning Mr said, 'Get the rickyard gates open - the threshers coming. Move yourself tomorrow morning boy, we will be threshing all day.' I was not going to ask about the loss of milk in the udder as I would have to milk earlier. There was no way I could move myself faster any other way. Next morning I could hear the steam engine chuntering away.

The man must have been in early and when I came out from breakfast several other men were arriving and Mr shouting 'Come on, get the thatch off. We have no time to waste.' But they were already doing it and, I could be wrong, but it seemed to me they slowed down, except one man, tall built like a bundle of bean poles. He had no laces in his boots, grubby black trousers, a vest and jacket to match. As I watched fascinated he was tearing the thatch off and throwing it in all directions. When all was ready, he jumped up on the tractor for the job of feeding the sheaves of wheat in the top. But the driver said no, he was to pitch sheaves from the rick to the thresher and someone else would do the feeding. It seems he was a manic without the depressive. So he would be shouting for more sheaves whilst ramming them in until he jammed the whole thing up.

When we got started my job was at the rear, where the corn came out, there was four chutes where the grain came out, each with a shutter, and the job was to hook sacks on and open the shutters to let the corn flow into the sacks. When a sack was full it was already resting on the ground and had to be unhooked, wrestled over to a pair of scales and weighed and added to or taken from to the correct weight of two and a quarter hundredweight, two hundred and fifty two pounds (or one hundred and twenty six kilos) and the top stitched up and put to one side. Oh, and if you had not enough to do you had to clear away the threshed straw that was constantly coming out overhead. Mr did come and help me a bit, but I noticed that when he did a sack he carefully put it under the straw. Perhaps he was protecting it from the sun?

At the end of the day, with two ricks of wheat done, we were all clearing up the loose straw and the men were joking about. One said to the manic 'You don't want to let that London boy get near your little maid, I wouldn't let him near my old tom cat. At that be the truth he be a right terror for the little maids he be.' I knew a maid was in dialect a young girl and thinking a chance would be a fine thing, I laughed. But he was not laughing, he came straight at me with his pitchfork saying 'You leave my little maid alone!' Somehow the handle of my pitchfork got in a tangle with his legs and as he dived into the straw, I took off, taking my pitchfork with me, to get the cows in.

Mum was right they had small lives and what was a joke to them was downright dangerous. I went cautiously to the rick-yard next morning. He was there but he appeared not to see me and during the day one or other of the men dropped back to help me and one said it were funny seeing him dive in the straw like that. I said he was a menace. 'Not at all', he said, 'he forgot that as soon as you were out of sight.' So I thought I would put a stop to this and said, 'I know something funnier, if he had hurt me and I pushed my pitch fork through his throat and got hung for it, wouldn't that be funny?' I received some very odd looks from that bunch the rest of the day.

One morning Mr said to Mrs 'We will be out all morning striking the sheep.' I could think of all sorts of striking but I would wait and see what this one was. So we set off with the big penknife and a jam jar full of what they called blue stone. Now we had used this before, he had made up a solution of these copper sulphate crystals which he poured over a heap of seed wheat on the barn floor and we turned it backwards and forwards like mixing cement which, I was told when I asked, was to keep the wireworm and leather jackets from damaging the wheat when it was sown - so what use would it be to sheep. Soon found out. It was getting more lanolin on your trousers catching and upending sheep and Mr would trim the overgrown hooves and occasionally find foot-rot or a maggot had eaten its way into the sole, that was evicted and the blue stone pushed into the damage. So blue stone was a cure-all. I was not to know then but I was to use it to good effect years later when I had stock of my own.

When all the crops were planted the pace of work slowed down, of course the routine work went on, but every other job seemed less fraught. I did upset him a bit when we were sowing the turnips because again it was not explained that my job was to look in the hopper from time to time to make sure that the seeds were evenly spread throughout and, of course, I did not, so when he stopped the horse and came back, one end of the hopper was empty, and he exploded 'Are all the boys in London as much of a trial as you?' I was beyond caring.

One day as he went through his mail he burst out 'Look at that I received twenty-one shillings a ton for my wheat. Things really are improving I'm buying a shearing machine. We will start shearing next week!' Soon after two men arrived with an oak post and set it in a hole they had cut in the barn floor and clamped the top to a roof truss then a man arrived in a van bringing the shearing machine and fitted it to the post and connected it to the overhead pulley system. Then Mr opened a door in the back wall of the barn and there, in a lean-to shed, was a horizontal barn engine. I was amazed at the secret society I was working in - not once had he ever mentioned that engine. I had been kibbling barley by hand when the grinder could have been driven by the engine; I only supposed I was cheaper than the paraffin it would have used.

About this time he said I'll pay you by the month, it will be easier. I did not bother to answer I knew Mum was not short of money and she was bartering sunlight soap for many of her needs. She had bought a salvage crate from the insurance loss adjusters. Soap was in short supply and farmers' wives needed it so it was exchanged gradually for milk, butter, cream, pork, mutton, fruit and veg so they were well fed.

Shearing commenced with the horseman and me bringing the sheep one at a time and Mr using his new machine - which turned out not to be as simple as expected, because the technique was totally different and several sheep got grazed and he was beginning to lose his temper, saying 'It's slower than hand shears!' but he gradually improved and at dinner time he was telling his wife how marvellous it was.

After dinner we got through the rest of the flock, but it took two of us to get the ram in and to hold him still and when Mr had finished him he broke free. I jumped up on a corn bin, so he charged Mr who ran out of the door.

It had been arranged for them to be dipped at a local farm a while later, I think to let the grazes heal, we set off - the flock filling the lane. It was possible to move stock on the roads back then because there were so few motor vehicles around anyway. Mr was in front to turn the flock in the right direction and there were three of us following, the ram, me and the dog, with the ram behaving himself because I had the dog. The flock was going round a bend and there was an Austin Seven. The sheep started passing on both sides and, as they pushed their way through the car was rocking from side to side, and the driver gave a hoot. That panicked the sheep and the ram pushed his way through and charged. I saw him rise up and strike at the car. The rest of the flock flowed by and when they were through the ram followed, as I went by the driver was fuming and shouted at me, but my intermittent deafness had kicked in - but I did wonder about the water trickling onto the lane.

We eventually arrived at the farm I did not utter word about the car and Mr did not ask. The sheep were put in a big pen and I was to stand on the edge of the dip, which was a concrete lined ditch with a ramp each end leading down into this evil smelling liquid. I was given a long ash pole that had a natural crutch at the end, which I was to use to push the sheep, momentarily, completely under after which they scrambled out the other end where they stood draining and an old chap would let them out when they had. I soon realised why I had been given this job because some sheep jumped in the dip and the one with the pole got splattered with the liquid. As I duly pushed them under I noticed that their eyes and nostrils closed and that was amazing, then they opened again as they bobbed up. Then suddenly it was the ram's turn – he tried to go along the ledge between the dip and the fence. I jammed the pole across and he had to go in and he did a mad dash for the other end, so I pushed him under and there were bubbles and he struggled until Mr shouted to 'Let him up boy' and he burst to the surface, scrambled up the ramp and charged the old chap working the gate. I thought 'Hello? I must be improving - I did not get a 'damn boy' that time. After a few more ewes I heard one of the hands say 'how about the young tup Master?' and he replied, 'Yes he is getting a bit scabby.' I knew that tup meant ram and, as we had not got a young tup, so this bucolic joke meant me so I ran at the old chap with the pole. I kept the pole until we were well down the lane, and I threw it over a hedge.

After this the ram was separated from the ewes and the lambs were weaned off and put in a field on their own to fatten.

Chapter 28 bikes and emergencies

One morning Mr said, 'We are going to Okehampton cattle market today after breakfast, we will go by bike.' So I got my front wheel and as I was fixing it on he said, 'I'll ride yours - you have mine,' which was an old-fashioned affair and the wheel bearings would make cracking noises. I was not having any of that treatment on my bike so I rode off on mine quickly.

When we were riding along the main road he said, 'You ride way behind me.' So I did, thinking 'he doesn't want to be seen with me on a better bike than him.' On the brow of the hill there was a garage called Rubys and he put his bike in there leaning against the doors, which were wide open, where there were a few other bikes already. It seemed nobody rode down into Okehampton - I supposed that brakes would not be sufficient on that hill. When I saw him come out of the garage I went in and asked a mechanic working there if there was somewhere else I could put mine. He gave one look and said, 'Yes son, put it in the back of the garage behind that motor,' adding, 'if I had a beautiful bike like that I would not want to put it in that heap, and there will be more laid up against them before the morning's out as it's market day.'

When I came out, Mr was half way down the hill so I went on, thinking how nice it was to chat to a friendly stranger. I did not tell him my true reason for wanting a different place. When we finally arrived at the cattle market there were cattle tied to the fence around the sale ring and when he saw a vacant place he said, 'Stand there and do not let anybody use it,' and off he went and came back with a cow and calf I had not seen before and tied it to the rails and said, 'Watch her,' and went off.

Several men came and took cows away and I made sure no-one tried to take the cow I was watching and then Mr came back and, as he was untying the cow, he said, 'Damn boy is it beyond your capabilities to keep the calf away from her udder?' and went off and a few minutes later I heard the auctioneer shout 'The vendor of this lot asked me to tell you that his useless London boy has let the calf get at the near rear quarter' – and then him chanting away and the bang of his stick on the board and she was sold.

Mr brought her back and tied her up – he was looking quiet pleased with himself and without saying a word went off again so I still watched the cow until a man came along and untied the cow. I asked him where he thought he was going with the cow and he ignored me so I followed and when he tried to get it up the ramp of a cattle wagon I snatched a stick off someone and jumped up on the ramp to stop him. Suddenly Mr was there shouting 'Get off that ramp - the gentleman has bought the cow!' and half the market seemed to explode with laughter. Mr said to the buyer 'Sorry about that it's the sort of thing I have to put up with.' Mr did not mention it again and he still looked happy. It left me to wonder if there was something wrong with that near rear quarter. Mr seemed in high spirits as he strode up the hill to Rubys, and when I arrived he was looking through the bikes. I walked past him and retrieved mine. The mechanic nodded towards Mr and grinned. I thanked him, thinking he had sussed that one out.

Mr had bought-in some young cattle heifers, that is young females before their first calf, and steers, that is castrated bulls. One of the heifers was a bit smaller than the rest. I had heard Mr comment about it sometime later, we had an early dinner and Mr and Mrs and the child went off in the motor. I had plenty to do and was happy on my own.

Later that afternoon I heard a lot of bellowing from the young cattle so I went to see what was up, to find the steers chasing the small heifer around and she had a calf head sticking out of her rear. I did not think to get help from a neighbour so, after a lot of running about, I got the heifer into another field. I did not know if it was up for hay or not, and eventually she lay down, but when I tried to feel for the calf's front legs she tried to rise so I took my belt off and strapped one front hoof to the opposite side rear. The calf's eyes were shut and mouth wide open. I soon found one front leg was back but, after a lot of pushing and straining, I got it forward and out the calf came. I could not swing it, so pressed on its ribs and blew into its nostrils and it gave a sneezing cough and shook its head, so I dragged it round to her head, took my belt off and lay there looking at the sky, waiting for the shivering to stop.

When I went back to the yard the horseman was there he said, 'You're later getting the cows in.' So, though I could have done with a drink, off I went and the cows were waiting at the gate and as I was letting them out Mr arrived got out of his car saying 'Those cows should have been in twenty minutes ago - go to sleep did you?' I ignored him. He then said, 'Don't walk away when I am talking to you!' but before he could carry on I said, 'I have spent the afternoon pulling a calf of that little heifer and before I forget - I did it in the standing grass. Now if you do not mind I am going milking,' and I followed the cows.

After tea he said, 'Where is the heifer now?' 'I told you in the hay field.' 'You should have brought it in and put it in the loose box!' I was getting fed up by now so I responded 'What? And be late with the milking?' Off he went and I finished off the dough cake and cream - much to Mrs' dismay. I believe all that tantrum was because he had to spend the afternoon visiting her parents.

Later I asked Mr Penwarden what would be the result of a young heifer getting in calf, he said that would be the worst thing that could happen as it would not grow anymore - it was useless - a loss, and asked 'Where did this happen?' I was not going to say because these people did not need telephones for word to get round. So I asked 'How about wild cattle?' The reply was, 'They be different,' and I was none the wiser.

Chapter 29   haymaking, harvest and disputes

Time moved slowly onto haymaking. Some bright spark came up with 'double summer time' which began on May 4th 1941, so I was still a month away from my fifteenth birthday. I had to have an old alarm clock because the cows stayed on the old time and everything else the new. I thought it was a plot to get me working longer hours. There were some farmers who would have none of it and carried on at the old time but their wives kept a clock on the new so they knew when to go out to catch a bus into Okehampton.

Haymaking got underway - the turning was still by hand, outside help came into do that, they were farm labourers' wives earning a bit extra. And when it came to saving it, it was raked up in lines by a horse drawn rake, which you sat on top of and at your right hand was a long lever so when the horse went forward and the rake was full you stopped the horse, leaned forward, grabbed the lever and pulled back to raise the rake to deposit the hay. So the first snag was my arm was not long enough so I had to raise myself out of the seat and pull, now it may have been my lack of weight or strength or the crude engineering but it was a struggle. So now I'm in this precarious position, I had to tell the horse to go forward, and as it did so the jerk caused me to let go the handle, so down went the rake taking half of the previously gathered hay. It felt about an hour and a half later before I had more or less got the hang of it except, it was pointed out to me, the lines were not very straight. After tea break I was told to put

Bess in the rake as the other horse was needed elsewhere, so we started in a different field and Bess and I took off and when the rake was full I raised it, gave a click and she moved gently forward and I let go the leaver and on we went depositing the hay about twenty feet apart. I got a surprise when we went back, without a word she stopped exactly right. Somebody said, 'Nice straight rows lad'. I still do not understand why the precision was needed when half an hour later they were swept into the rick.

Soon after I learnt more of her skills. I was told to take a wagon load of hay out of a field with Bess in the shafts. I had not driven a wagon before so we headed for the gate and as we approached it Bess stopped dead and would not move until I flipped her rump with the rein ends so she started off and promptly tore the gatepost out with a front wheel. When I got to the rick Mr said, 'After you have finished tonight I want that post put back good and solid.' I said nothing but I knew it was not in solid before. When I was unharnessing her the horseman said, 'She has taken more wagons through gates than you have ever seen, she don't need steering towards a gate she knows where she be going, so sit back with loose reins and she will sail through.' And over the next few weeks I wondered why I needed to be there at all.

As the weeks settled down into a sort of rhythm, the weather was good and the corn was ripening, we began refurbishing the rick-bed ready for the harvest. Unlike hay-ricks the corn beds were raised on those granite mushrooms that are now sold as garden ornaments - their real job was to prevent rats from climbing into the rick. On top of the mushrooms were laid ash poles both ways and on top of that a thick bed of thorn and bramble, saved from when the hedges were cut. I had to marvel at the ingenuity and their 'nothing wasted life-style' to use a modern expression. I now think my loner attitude saw me through this period. The farming community did not seem to discuss anything beyond stock crops or weather and although they did not say much I looked forward to seeing the different faces of the harvest help.

Our corn harvest started in a peculiar way – as we enacted out a process that, it turned out, had been going on for hundred years or so. One morning after breakfast we went out and the horseman was waiting with the pair of horses hitched to a reaper band, with Bess in full harness between the shafts of the wagon, and two casual labourers.

We then set off up the hill and into the drive of another farm (run by Mr's older brother) but as we passed through the farmyard we had to walk leading the horses. The farmer, his wife and at least six hands were standing there scowling at us and I could feel the waves of resentment coming off them. There was something really cold about the whole affair. Then we went up a lane and the horseman took the reaper through a gate, while I waited with Bess and the casuals started making sheaves out of the corn tying them with corn stalks. The corn they were tying had already been cut by someone with a scythe to the width needed so the reaper would not be spoiling it to get a start. The reaper got going and Mr led, Bess following it, while I, and the labourers, loaded the sheaves on. The field was not very big and in one big wagonload it was finished - but we had to go all over it and pick up every last bit of straw and when we left the two casuals followed close behind picking up even the smallest bits of straw that fell from the wagon.

We passed back through the hostile stares as we had on the way in and back to our farm for lunch. After which we emptied the wagon in a meadow recently cut for hay. The sheaves then were stood on their but ends in sixes, so the wind could flow through and dry them with the ears of corn up in the sun to ripen.

I gradually found out that the whole charade had been going on for a hundred years and, though nobody seemed to know why, the rules were; if one farmer stopped, because of the inconvenience and the waste of time and the poor harvest due to the size of the field and the mono crop - it always had to be grain, or the other farmer objected or obstructed because of the disruption caused by the horseman going in and out ploughing, dung spreading, harrowing, tilling and then the harvesting, the transgressor would have to pay the other an undisclosed sum - but commonly thought to be a large sum. Also, it was commonly thought, that if they were to come to some agreement and stop competing, then said sums would be payable to the land owner. Little wonder that Mr was on such a short fuse.

All the grain was ready to harvest but the weather turned dull and damp without actually raining - real Dartmoor stuff. If it did not dry up quickly so the harvest could carry on the danger was that the ears of corn could sprout and be ruined. While this was going on a man arrived, by the state of his car obviously a farmer, Mr came out to meet him and took him to look at a cow in the loose box. It had been there about a week and Mr had been milking it and putting the milk in the churn so I was unaware of what it was giving so when I was passing them to go to tea the man said, 'And you say she's giving four gallons?' Mr said, 'Ask the boy he takes care of her.' The man did say something but I went deaf and kept going. I heard the car go and Mr shouted at me 'When I ask you to confirm what I say don't walk off.' I was about to say 'I don't tell lies and I won't tell them for anyone else.' But I did not get a chance as he grabbed my shoulders. I realised I was going to get shaken and, at the same time, my right boot cracked into his shin twice. He let go and stood there staring. I waited for what would come next but there was nothing so I turned away to go in, looking for something I could grab if he moved.

Again nothing, so I slid into my place behind the table. Mrs started putting my cooked tea on the plate and completely spontaneously I said, 'I am really hungry,' and to my surprise she turned back to the frying pan and put some more on it. I thanked her, but I was thinking 'What now? The sack? No, I have really done it this time! It'll probably be a car-ride into Okehampton copper station. Charged. Magistrate. Court. Borstal. After all what else could you expect from a London boy, vicious breed that they are? My only defence was I was brought up not to suffer bullying and to retaliate and then on the other hand he did not actually get to shake me - he may only have been going to tell me off.'

In the few minutes in which that had passed through my head I realised I had cleared my plate and the door opened and Mr came in but, instead of sitting at the table, he sat in an old wooden armchair by the fire. Mrs looked at him a bit puzzled and he started to roll his trousers up. I heard her give a gasp and there were two awful welts and one was bleeding. She got a bowl of warm water threw a bit of salt in and started bathing it and asked 'Whatever happened dear?' And without look up he said, 'I slipped on the steps and could I have a cup of tea.' She looked at him in wonder he had actually asked quietly, so I got on with the dough cake and cream and she said, 'The way that boy is eating I think he is growing,' but he never answered.

After I went up and finished the evening jobs and when I went in at last they had gone to their own part of the house. I sat in the chair for a while giving thought to what could happen next. There was no telephone so he could not call the law. But he could take me in to Okehampton cop shop tomorrow and get me charged with assault, result borstal and the birch - the enemy of East End boys. Nightmare. So I went out and talked it over with Bess. Naturally she made no comment. So I went to bed and found less comfort than usual. Next morning I got up and milked as usual and I was just finishing off Brooksy, the house cow, when the doorway darkened and he muttered something but the tone was different and it was not the usual 'time's getting on'. And at breakfast he looked across the table towards me and I thought here it comes, if the mentions the law I'm off - catch a lift to Exeter and volunteer for the army. But he said, 'If this weather holds we will start the harvest and I think we will get started on the winter oats first.' I sat there like a dummy with a fork full of fried potatoes halfway to my mouth thinking I must be hallucinating. But on he went, 'And I would think that Bess is too distended now to go in the wagon and it would be better if you worked her in the load cart with the shafts as low as you can get them.' I gave a horseman's nod to that, still in a trance. He must be up to something. It must be the shock of someone retaliating. It could never have happened before as most farm workers were still pulling their forelocks with a 'Yes Master.'

The weather became quite warm and more labour arrived and the harvest was at last under way. On the first day I looked towards the gate and Mrs was coming with three other ladies carrying big baskets with the white cloths over. I realized it was tea time and we were going to work on after as double British Summer time meant it was warm and light until eight o'clock. The men sat down and the ladies started handing out beautiful sandwiches with ham in them. The taste was wonderful. I did look round to see if I had been given the same as the men and so I had, and there were big billy-cans of tea too. I guessed the hams that had been hanging on the kitchen beams were gone. As the men got started again Mr came to me and said, 'I think you could go back and milk now and come back after.' So off I went back, helping the ladies carry the baskets.

When I returned the horseman was taking the binder to the next field to start next day and the men and Mr were standing the last of the sheaves up in stooks in straight rows across the field and one of them said, 'That be a heavy crop Master'. Mr was pleased. But I thought the old git only wanted a bigger share of the sandwiches. I wished I had thought of it. When I went in the hams weren't hanging up where they had been, as I had thought.

Chapter 30   Bess!!

The harvest went on and when all the reaping was done we started on the first field again, by now the sheaves were completely dry and the horseman with the wagon and me with Bess in the load cart started carrying the sheaves to the rick-yard where three men were building the ricks. One man helped me to load the cart and two men and the horseman loading the wagon with another on top who built the load. And day after day it went on with big ham sandwiches for tea.

I was happy working with Bess though she really did bulge out over the shafts each side and on the last day, with only a few loads left, the field was fairly steep so we were picking up the load straight up and down the hill turning on the flatter land at the top and bottom. The cart was almost full when I noticed two sheaves lying off to my side, probably fallen from a previous load, so I went to fetch them but I heard a crack and looked back. Bess was following me - bringing the cart diagonally across the slope. I shouted but the cart was already tipping down-hill and she was straining to hold it. I tried to get her turned up hill again and the load started to slip off down-hill which relieved Bess of some of the strain but she was already too far beyond upright and started to go down. The shaft she had been leaning on snapped and down she went, rear first, but gently because she was still attached to what I was still holding. Her ears laid back and I knew she was going to lash out at the cart. By some sort of instinct I knelt down, laid my arm across her neck, rubbing my hand across her muzzle and whispering in her ear, how sorry I was and to keep still, and she relaxed and nibbled at my palm. I was trying to get her bridle off and someone said, 'You keep her calm son, we will take care of the rest' and there seemed to be hands everywhere getting her harness off and dragging the cart away. She even lifted her head for me as they took her bridle off and she flicked her ear. I then realised I had been crying into it, and I was told to stay with her head and encourage her to get up and she tried, and each time they pushed sheaves under her back, and after many attempts she got her legs under her and a ton of horse stood up! I was still talking to her when she gave me a nudge that sat me on the stubbles. Someone laughed and then they were all at it. I think with sheer relief - and they had something new to yarn about.

I walked her slowly back to her stable and rubbed her down and gave her a drink and a handful of oats. By the time I left her the field was cleared, the cart was in the cart shed and the men had gone. I told the horseman I had given her some oats, he said, 'She deserved some and so do you, if you had not kept her quiet with your talk she would have kicked the cart to bits and as like as not strained her ham-string or fractured her fetlocks.' All of which was gibberish to me. Then he went on to say, 'And then she would never get up.' and I had a flash-back to the one in poplar high street and blood running down the gutter. I had to leave the stable quickly and, as I turned towards the milking parlour, totally forgetting the cows were still out, I saw Mr was bringing them in. They went into their stalls and the chains were put around their necks but Mr said, 'Come in now lad, Mrs has got tea ready early and we will do the milking after, there is no hurry.' (No hurry! I must be dreaming).

I don't know if it was a celebration for the harvest-in but tea was like a dinner and instead of dough cake there was a lardy cake. I had never seen one of these before and when she put it on the table it was like a very open textured loaf but glistening with fat and you could see the white fat in the creases and loaded with dried fruit I began to wish I had not had so much to eat before it arrived. Mr was in a very affable mood and he told Mrs, 'The cart had tipped over and luckily Bess had fallen up hill and the boy knelt down and talked to her and she stayed still until we cleared away and he coaxed her to rise and she seems fine.' And just as I was thinking 'I've done all right for a change' as he had not even mentioned the broken shaft, he shattered my feeling of pleasure by adding, 'Of course she may abort the foal so we will have to keep an eye on her.' I think my heart dropped into my boots - when would the constant anxiety end? Was farming always like this or is it just me?

I don't know about his part in the keeping an eye on her but I went out and spent time with her before I went to bed just to talk about things and give her a light grooming and I got up even earlier to see how she was and have a chat. I used to sit in her manger, and one morning I awoke to a clattering of buckets, it was the horseman giving the other horses a drink, I had fallen asleep in the manger and had to scramble to start the milking. I don't know whether he told Mr but I was told that Bess was out of danger now and we could relax. She would not be worked anymore until after the foal was born but would need gentle exercise when I could fit it in, I just was thinking 'great!' when he said, of course the foal may be crippled and useless and would have to be put down. I was not useless - but had been born crippled - but he was not to know that so I let him wallow in his own pessimism.

Over the next few weeks we helped other farmers get their harvests in and I saw the same men that had come to help Mr get his in, and sure enough, tea time out came the women with the thick ham sandwiches. Mr was working like a labourer and a few days later as we sat down for tea one old chap sat by me and said, 'I know you – you're that poor little cripple lad that used to bide with Mrs Taylor at Taw Green Mill - you were some relation I believe.' I thought he obviously knows so I won't deny it so I said, 'She and my gran are sisters.' 'And you are all right now are you?' he asked. To which I replied, for all the earwiggers, 'Of course, and as good as anyone else.' He said, 'I don't doubt, you got that mare back on her feet they do say.' So there goes another London boy tale.

Finally the harvests were over, the horseman got on with the ploughing and one morning some men and women arrived with what looked like a slatted stretcher on short legs and other tools. And then a large pig arrived, I think from Mr's younger brother and sister that ran the farm in the valley bottom – whether it was one from the piglets we'd caught-up and Mr had taken off before, I do not know, but it was duly killed and the blood was caught and carried indoors. The pig was then laid on the stretcher and boiling water thrown over it and all the bristles scraped off, then it was hung up and disembowelled, cut up and carried indoors. The whole process went like magic and the men were packed up and gone scarcely saying a word, indoors the women were working equally smoothly washing all the small intestines through with warm salt water which were then put to soak in brine, to use as sausage skins, everyone working away methodically with scarcely a word and by lunch time they were finished, you would hardly have known there had been a pig there at all.

How many London people could do that and so efficiently? And they call country people slow. The hams went into a brine tank to replace the new ones now hanging on the beam which were for next years harvest - so the ones just going in the brine were for two years' time. My dinner that day was the usual fried spuds but with hogs pudding (chopped up pork and oats wrapped up in a piece of stomach lining neatly sewn up with sinews) as big as my fist and fried, of course, and just think, it was walking about just a few hours before - lovely.

Chapter 31   sheep and 'mother'

Our time now seemed to be taken-up by tidying up the jobs not done because of the hectic harvest time and I was sent to look at the sheep that Mr had been seeing in the mornings while I was milking. They were now grazing a field about two miles away. When I got there the sheep ran together in a bunch. Unusual. It made them difficult to count, so I moved behind a big bramble patch out of their sight so they would spread out again and while I waited I started to get the smell of dead sheep, so I went further in and gazed into the brambles, where I saw two sheep that had been partly eaten alive at least two days before.

By now the sheep had spread out enough to count and I made it three short. I peddled back to the farm and Mr said, quite pleasantly, 'Did you have a puncture?' because of the time taken. So I informed him politely that my count had made it three short and that I'd found two of them rammed into the brambles with their backsides eaten and while he stood there, no doubt trying to remember when he had last seen them, I went and found two shovels and wheeled out both bikes - then he came to and instead put them in the car.

When we arrived I showed him the two and said, 'I will go and find the other one.' We then heard two voices and an obvious pair arrived dressed in smart tweed suits and carrying baskets - they had been picking blackberries in the field. I looked at Mr's face and decided to go - but before I was out of earshot I heard the man say 'There is a dead sheep over there

– shouldn't it have been buried by now?' and I went deaf before the roar of rage that would come.

I found and disposed of the sheep and went back. The couple were gone - but there were blackberries scattered on the ground and I could only assume he had made them tip them out, he was digging furiously so I joined in and without word we rolled the other two in and covered them.

We gently eased the rest of sheep out of the field, noticing that some had lumps of wool torn out of their rumps, so when we had them home we treated the wounds and I had to put the old sheep dog in the loose box because she was the last thing the sheep needed to see until they recovered. Then Mr put his gun in the car and drove off and did not return until getting dark. He was out again next morning before it was light and home again late, and off again next morning but was back by ten. Mrs cooked him a big breakfast. He was in a better mood then and cleaned his gun

I was finding his new softer attitude disconcerting. He used to try to tell me farm jokes; like the farmer caught his boy asleep on the grass and said to the boy what are you doing down there, to which the boy replied catching moles master so the master said how many have you caught then the boy replied when I have caught this one sir and three more that will be four sir. And then he would laugh uproariously but I did not see the funny side after all the boy's arithmetic was sound....

Autumn wore on and we were busy filling the hayloft ready for the cows coming in for the winter. There was a woman coming in and helping Mrs get the meals and gradually the Mrs only appeared teatime, bringing the little girl. We had brought in a cartload of flat-poll cabbages for the cows to munch on, these cabbages were nearly a meter across and weighed between six and eight kilos and they got one each after morning milking.

One day Mr said, 'Do not give Brooksy any more flat poll.' Two days later he told me he now had a son and that he weighed eight and a half pounds! He stood there obviously expecting some sort of congratulations. So I said, 'He'll soon be able to help with the milking then,' and while he stood there trying to work out whether it was a joke or not I was thinking 'There was I wondering if she was ill,' because Mrs was thinner than a half starved sixteen-year-old East End girl, and if that baby was the declared weight I don't know how she hid it. I also now knew why Brooksy got no cabbage because the baby would be fed on the house-cow milk so I started a new method –I only put seven cabbages in the barrow and by starting at the door, gave the cows one each this made sure that when I got to the end the barrow was empty and Brooksy got none.

A few mornings later Mr came into the shippen in a rage and said a doctor had been there nearly all night as the baby had been very ill and he went on shouting 'Isn't there anything you can do right? You have given Brooksy cabbage and I expressly told you not to!' and pushed past me to look in her manger. In his temper he forgot that you spoke to an animal by sliding your hand along its back so it is aware you are there, so when bent forward to see in her manger her head, with its wide horns, swung around and the point of the horn cracked into the bone above his right eye socket. He came staggering out but, of course, there was no cabbage in the manger. I watched him cross the yard weaving a bit from side to side, twice he started to raise his hand to his eye but rammed it down again, not giving into the pain, I did wonder whether the eye socket was fractured. I knew he would not see a doctor, especially after the expense of a doctor there most of the night before. I put the cows out, because we had not much rain yet and ground was still firm so they wouldn't damage the turf, a decision usually made by him.

I went in and he was sitting at the table, almost rigid, with his breakfast in front of him. He had started but I think the pain of moving his jaw was too much, so I went and got him some hot sweet tea as he had had a shock, and for the very first time I heard him use the word 'thank you'. The woman gave me my breakfast. He slowly got up and went down the other end. The woman asked what had happened, I replied 'I do not know.' I did not want that information to fly around the county. As for me, if he had calmly asked me about the cabbage, if he had only a bit of trust in me and if his explosive temper hadn't made him disregard a rule that he had learned from the cradle, it wouldn't have happened. I had no sympathy, but I did wonder if they boiled the milk for the baby. I could not ask because that would infer criticism and I knew what his view of that would be.

His eye became worse, the bottom lid sagged down and the black and purple bruising spread across his forehead and below his cheekbone, but I noticed he never left the farm.

We went into a big clean up and repair activity and gradually his eye improved and everything went back to normal - or what passed for it. Then on a day when I was putting out straw chaff, chopped for the horses, the barn door opened and he was helping an elderly lady over the step followed by two smartly dressed men, one with a clipboard, and she walked slowly round looking everywhere though she looked right through me as I carried on. I realised that she must be the owner and this was an annual inspection, and the other two were a steward and his clerk. Now I knew what all the big tidy up was about, I would have liked to have left but they were between me and the door, and finally she arrived at the sheep-shearer and slowly looked up and down the oak post. She tapped it with her stick and asked 'Where was this cut from?' He dropped his head and replied 'From the woods, Mother,' and she turned towards him and said 'I do not remember a request to remove a tree - and I certainly did not give permission.' I so wished I could escape at that minute, because he was mentally on his knees as he said, 'Sorry Mother, I forgot.' She nodded at the steward and his clerk wrote something down and off they went for further inspections. What a vicious old woman to humiliate her son in front of others, including me. What that post cost him on top of his rent I wouldn't know but I do know that woman knew about the post before she came. I now understood what was driving this man to build up a fortune in dealing, to escape this family trap, and get a farm of his own, and he had not been able to go dealing with his eye in the state it was in.

He began to get in a more pleasant mood and we worked together well but nothing was discussed so all I saw or thought about was trapped in my head. Mr started to talk about getting a tractor, not to me but in short statements at meal times, saying things like 'they don't eat anything when the ground is too hard with frost or too wet.' 'They can plough five acres a day where a man and two horses can only manage one.'

I had heard these arguments before my uncle Bill Mallet and his brother used to discuss it at length and the conclusion was always that all your equipment would have to be converted to be towed by tractor; that some of the machinery could only be towed at horse pace such as reaper binders and seed drills. Both these men were rabbit trappers supplying the London market, with around three hundred a day, and working their market gardens, supplying Exeter. It was always a mystery to me when they found time to sleep. So I knew both sides of this argument but said nothing, though I knew somebody who would be saddened by the loss of the horses. One was usually kept for jobs not worth starting the tractor for, such as fetching in hay and mangles or cabbage and other odd jobs, and that would be Bess.

Chapter 32   pony and tractor

Then a surprise! Mr came home with a pony, it seemed to me to be a funny colour. But when Mrs came out to see he said it was a strawberry roan and when I looked closely it had individual hairs in its coat white, reddish-brown and a sprinkling of black. And it was so fat there were dimples along its back where the skin is attached to the backbone. I thought 'What does he want it for unless we were going to eat it?' I still think that now when I see a fat pony I always imagine what a nice freezer full it would make. He went onto say it had been on its own all summer on grass and had done no work but we will soon get the weight off, she can have Bess' stall and a handful of hay a day and water and the boy can do that. I thought that's typical, he buys a fat pony and I am the one to starve it thin. Then he went on to say, 'It is not known if it is broken. Me and the boy can do that in the evening.' But it was okay - when he told me to jump up on it - it did not move thank goodness.

A few weeks later, when she was thinner, he sent me down to Taw Green blacksmith to get her shoed. I was to walk her down before the shoeing and he said I could ride her back. When I got to the blacksmith he was already shoeing a pair of Suffolks. He gave on look at the pony and said, 'I know that one – she's not been shod for years. I will have to remove a lot of hoof. I'm surprised she hasn't got hoof rot.'

While we awaited our turn I did wonder about all the Dartmoor ponies who are never shod, and then it was our turn and the instruction was 'You keep steady boy I don't want to be kicked all over the shop.' But she stayed calm even when the hot shoes were tried on and the smoke from the scorching hoof rose up around her head. When it was all completed I said, 'Thanks,' and he said, 'Thanks won't buy the baby a new bonnet.' That stopped me dead - I had not been given any money - I must have looked bewildered so he said, 'That's all right boy, you get on back,' so I tied the end of the lead rope to the other side of the halter thinking about the bucolic joke and jumped up on her back. And he said, 'Whoa you're never going to ride her without a bridle?' I gave him a wave and trotted off – there goes another London boy story.

I went round to Davoncourt to show Mum the pony and she was gently running her fingers through it's mane telling me of some jobs to do when I came back on Wednesday when Aunt Bess came to the door and said, 'Your Grandfather was a cavalry man and he sat up straighter than that.' Good old Aunt Bess, full of praise as usual - I gave her a wave and trotted off.

About half way back, and after I passed Wybets farm, I was riding the pony slowly uphill and there was some very light smoke drifting across the road which unsettled her a bit and, perhaps, I should have got off and led her but we were just clear of the smoke when two men bobbed up and blew through their hands like hunting horns - and the pony took off and, because I did not have a proper bridle with a bit, there was no way I could control her. I could hear the cheers and laughter behind me but she was really running now and knowing I had a T-junction coming I pulled her head round - and as we entered the T-junction round she went - if it had been a car we would have been on two wheels! Then, still at full-speed, down the track to the farm and straight across the farmyard, heading for her stalls, when she started to slow up, thank goodness, because it was one step up to get in. She stopped and Mr said, 'Whatever possessed you boy? Galloping her like that you may have shaken the shoes loose!' I lost it a bit when I said, 'She should be trained not to take off when there is smoke and men blowing up like hunting horns. And it would have helped if we had a proper bridle.'

I could not believe it – he just stood there unable to reply to a farm boy answering back. I took her into her stall and the horseman, who had been in there all the time, came with a big grin on his face and said, 'Get her a bucket of warm water and I will rub her down and check her shoes.' I heard no more on that subject so I went into dinner and soon after she had a bridle and there was a saddle, but according to Mr I could not use that because I had no experience with riding and if I were to fall off and not get my foot out of the stirrup I would be dragged along with my head under the rear hooves. I accepted that was the reason why he would not let me use it. The only thing was, as I had no stirrups, I could not learn the bobbing up and down bit.

I took her out most evenings for a run and I found I could go round the sheep and the ram ignored us. I also soon found that I could not let her and Bess out together because she would circle round Bess and Bess would let fly with those hooves, once catching the edge of my right hand - for a while I thought it was broken. Whether she was jealous or just irritated with the pony I don't know but what I did know was that if she had hit the pony she would have killed it.

We seemed to drift into winter – the tractor arrived, a second-hand Fordson. It would have been a nightmare for health and safety with its great big back wheels which had two rows of teeth round each and when you sat on the seat, just the same – iron, these wheels with the teeth just about elbow height with a flimsy affair pretending to be a guard. And of course no antifreeze meant draining it when finished and refilling it before starting. As for starting on a frosty morning! No starter motor, just a big handle to try turning the big engine over with, after five minutes of which I was out of breath and sucking freezing air like broken glass. It was easy to see the advantage of grooming and feeding horses in a warm stable which then have an instant start on a word of command.

One day I was told to clean the inside of the car out. Being a farmer's car it had at one time or another had just about everything appertaining to farm work including sheep, calves and, at one time, a pig. So I set to and got a bucket of muck off the floor and with some warm water washed the leather seats - which I dried as best I could - and left the doors open to help dry them while I attempted to get the mud off the outside and out he came - all togged up. He gave one look, growled and pulled the old sheep dog out by the scruff of its neck. I had not seen it sneak in there – he grabbed some of the dirty hay stuff I had cleaned out of the car, gave the seats a bit of a rub, then drove the car round the front of the house. Out came Mrs carrying the baby boy in a lace christening gown and the little girl. I suppose it was none of my business where they were going so why tell me.

A few days before Christmas he said a screw had got lost out of the play-pen and I was to go down to their sitting room to look for it because I had younger eyes than them. He showed me the room and it had a nice wool carpet with a soft pile. I lifted out the toys but could not see it and an idea came to me. There was a small tin tray there which I picked up and dropped, working round the play-pen and after a while I heard a chink. Just as he said, 'That's a waste of time' I lifted the tray, felt in that small area of carpet and picked out the screw. He turned to Mrs and said, 'He must have seen it.' I said, 'I heard it.' 'Nonsense!' he said, so I asked him if he could hear bats sing as they fly in and out of the hay loft. He turned to his wife and said, 'That boy will be hearing voices in his head next.' But then she spoke, which was a rare event, and said, 'He found the screw dear', then he asked me what I did in the evenings. I said, 'I read.' He said, 'If you like you could come here in the evenings.' I thought it was cosy and so I said, 'Yes, please.' So night after night I went down, I always knocked on the door before I went in, and sat quiet reading and one evening he literally took the book from my hand and looked at it for a moment or two then said, 'What sort of story is that?' I replied, 'It's not a story but a history of Elizabeth's sailors given in three parts by a Russian professor to young navel seamen.' I offered him the book which was printed in the mid eighteen hundreds and, thankfully, he refused it and turned, looked at Mrs and said, 'Won't grow much corn knowing that will it?' and of course she had to agree.

As the days went by I went down to the parlour in the evenings and it's true to say it was not very comfortable. I would have been better off in the kitchen but seeing that he was making an effort to be different I resolved to stick it out. It had already been arranged that I should stay on the farm Christmas day because Mr and family were to spend the day with her parents. I would be off after milking on Boxing Day all day - but I would lose my half day Wednesday. So on Christmas Eve we were sitting there and he said, 'If you to go out to the shippen at half past eleven you'll see the cows kneel down at twelve o'clock.' I just could not help myself as the East End boy kicked in. I said, 'It's a pity you haven't any pigs - we would see them fly as well.' Mrs had a little giggle and he looked from one to the other – his face could not make out whether to be angry or laugh so I went on to say 'Ecclesiastical scholars cannot make up their minds what day it was let alone the hour, Bethlehem being to the East of us would make it more like half past ten.' He spluttered a bit then said, 'Where do you get all this nonsense?' My reply was, 'Before Hitler saw fit to bomb me out my home and destroy my family business I was a constant churchgoer and studied for confirmation gaining two prize books in the process. And no, I did not get confirmed, I would not because I could not see myself living by the ten commandments because Great Uncle George's prediction is coming true, I do not want a conscience.' They both sat there open mouthed staring. They had just had a look outside their own small bubble - I said, 'Goodnight,' and went off to bed.

After milking and breakfast they went off to her parents they seemed a bit quiet. I never even heard a Merry Christmas. The horseman came into feed and water the horses, but he had nothing much to say and went. I gave Bess her daily walk – she was getting very big now – she seemed to be glad to be back in her loose box after and we had a chat, which made me realise I was becoming quite reclusive. I took the pony out and went round the sheep, then spent the rest of the day in his big chair by the fire, reading and dozing, then heated up the bubble and squeak she had left me to eat. Just as I finished milking that evening they arrived home and by the time I gave the cows their last feed and went in she had tea laid and sitting in the middle of the table in all its glistening beauty was a lardy cake which I hailed with a 'Merry Christmas'. She giggled, and I noticed I got a large piece. Next morning I was out early to get all the feeding done before milking, which I did not want to start too early, can't have a few fluid ounces less in the churn can we, went in and Mrs was just getting breakfast. She looked a bit surprised when as soon as it was ready I scoffed it, said cheerio and was out the door; I retrieved my bike and was off.

Chapter 33   rams, cards and a foal

I was soon back at Devon Court. It seemed Mum had delayed Christmas - and breakfast was ready so I had another one for dinner! Mum had got a big old boiling hen and, when plucked and drawn, she had put it in a big tin which she filled with cider and put the tin in a big saucepan full of water and it had simmered on the stove for a week and at dinner time it was so tender she didn't need to carve it, the delicious meat was falling off the bones. Somehow Mum had made a Christmas pudding and served it with clotted cream.

Mum said Dad had written to say the raids had slowed down and consisted mainly of incendiary bombs and he and his crew with their trailer pump, normally pulled by a motor vehicle but with the lack of suitable drivers they had to pull the pump themselves, were busy. This must seem ridiculous in this day and age, but then few men could drive, incredible as it sounds, very few working men could even ride a bike let alone owned one. So the team used to push and pull the pump to the incident to save the property, so successful were these teams across London that Hitler began firing an explosive device to deter the fire fighters. Dad had said he would try to visit in a week's time.

So the day went happily on Mum had all sorts of little presents for Dorothy and had filled that bottle with port for Aunt Bess again. Amazingly there was a pair of Wellingtons for both Peter and me. The rest of the day passed happily and eventually my siblings went to bed and Aunt Bess said she had better go and lie down before she fell down. So Mum and I talked mainly about the future - Mum said we would survive but the going would be hard. She very much doubted whether we could get a business going again. The 'Queens' had been hit, she did not know how badly and chances of renting a large house was remote, mainly due to the amount of housing destroyed, and there never was enough housing in the first place. I set off back to the farm about eleven at night.

A few days later lambing started and it snowed and, to make matters worse, they were early because of the size of the Southdown ram. We took it in turns to be there all the time. I blessed my Wellingtons - I don't think I could have kept on going without them. Finally, all was done and he said at dinner 'I cannot remember ever having as hard a lambing as that.' I had to pinch myself to make sure I was alive and I had not dreamt it all - he must have known why.

Soon after, we awoke to deep snow and drifts, after I had got the milk up the road, and they were having breakfast, I put my head in the door and told him I was off to Davoncourt and that I would borrow a shovel, and was gone. Took me a while to get there - the front wheel stuck and I came off a few times. Mum and the family were not so badly snowed in as last time. Peter had cleared the porch and the outside pump, but it took a while to get it pulling again. Eventually they were comfortable and Mum had made a thick hot stew. I felt every mouthful sliding down.

When I returned to the farm I was asked, 'Was there not somebody at Davonourt who could shift a bit of snow?' I said, 'Oh yes, there is a seventy-year-old

Great Aunt, who had just been dug out of her own home, there's my Aunt, crippled from the age of five with polio, a boy aged eleven, a girl aged seven and my mother - of course, plenty of them.' He stood there just looking puzzled and I realised he was baffled by sarcasm. I just suppose nobody had ever used any on him before or did not dare.

Slowly the farming year got started. The first week of March it was reasonable weather and Bess was in the meadow and I saw her lay down and, something I never seen her do before, she laid her head and neck along her side and she heaved. I called in at the house to say I thought Bess was having her foal and was promptly told it's too early. I went back to the meadow just in time to see a cloud of steam go up - I went to her and there was the foal. I have seen smaller ponies and only half its back legs were clear. I caught hold of its front hooves and pulled it clear – its head was up and breathing. Good job I thought - you would need a crane to lift that on up and swing it. I can only describe the foal as the most beautiful thing I had ever seen. Mr and the horseman arrived and Mr said, 'Well what is it?' I was dumbfounded it was obvious, so I said, 'It's a foal,' but before he could explode the horseman lifted one back leg and said, 'Colt.' Mr said to me 'Well don't just stand there, get it on its feet!' so I took hold of its slimy neck but could not grip. 'No,' he said, 'lift it by its tail.' Just then Bess was getting to her feet. I took hold of its tail and heaved. It came up alright but gave a whickering sound, and Bess came fully up and laid her ears back - she was going to kick me away. Spontaneously I said, 'It's me Bess,' she relaxed and her ears went forward again. I had not noticed during those split seconds that the foal had kicked my shin, but it bruised it. Mr said, 'Things to do' a stock phrase of his and went off. The horse man stayed. When Mr was out of earshot he shook my hand and said, 'I have never seen a kick stopped with just a word before - a kick started is a kick delivered,' and I said, 'And a London boy goes home in a box?' His only comment was the usual 'Arrr.' Was it usual to lift a foal by its tail? If not - why endanger me? I still don't know.

Things became interesting after that - the colt had to be haltered - I know why I got that job. Every time I tried and he objected Bess only nudged me away. After a few days of trying, at odd times, finally it was on but I could only ever walk him as long as I had Bess on my other side, without her calming influence he would pull me over all over the place. It was surprising how strong he was getting.

The Southdown ram disappeared. I gave a silent cheer, and Mr got a couple of Devon close wool rams and they were quite tame and had horns that curled round flat against their heads. They were beautiful. I began calling them the 'Houdinis' - they constantly disappeared from wherever they were and had to be found, usually on neighbours land, and retrieved with apologies. I was getting fed up with it. I had enough to do without finding the gaps, some of which were so small it seemed impossible, and patching them up.

One morning they were gone. As usual I put my head in the kitchen door and shouted 'Houdinis have gone' When I went into breakfast he said, 'Found those rams yet?' I said, 'No, I have been milking and before you ask; I don't know - they don't confide in me.' He stared and spluttered and threw his fork down his on what was left of his meal. I said, 'Someone unloaded a load of trouble.' When I looked up Mrs was looking sad at me, shaking her head. Five minutes later I heard the pony gallop out of the yard - he was back about two hours later. A farmer about three miles away had them in a shed and we were to fetch them. We went and, in front of me, the farmer said he expected some compensation for the damaged spring wheat. I drifted away but something changed hands. We tied a bit of cord on their horns and led them away and the parting shot from the farmer was 'I think they be lazy too.' Walking them back to the farm I thought the way they got about and the thought crossed my mind that they were not too keen on the ewes - so dinner time I asked him what the farmer had meant about them being lazy - saying 'they look energetic enough to me.' Mrs' head came up and she was looking at him; I thought he was choking on his food, and I didn't get an answer that evening.

When I went down to the parlour I had hardly sat down when he said 'Instead of reading why not have a game of cards?' Now I dislike card games - Mum and Dad would play in the evening sometimes with visitors or when they visited someone, however, I thought it best to be sociable and agree, though thinking 'if he starts letting me win and then wants to play for my wages I'm out the door!' But, no, I never received a hand I could do anything with, even when I wracked my brains for anything my mother had tried to drum into it about cards. He was becoming quite jovial winning hands, and suddenly there it was - a good hand, I could hear mum saying 'good or bad hand keep a straight face' and I had three high trumps and three high of the other suits and I took hand after hand. The atmosphere changed and before he laid his last card he said, 'Can you take my last card?' I did not utter a word. He threw his last card down. I showed him mine and he stood up and shouted 'You young s***!' Mrs said something about waking the children. He said, 'He wouldn't tell me what he had!' - but I was already out of the door. If he was fed up with me being there I would be glad to go. Why go through all that charade if he wasn't playing properly - or was it that a peasant was not supposed to beat the master?

The two rams were kept in a loose box after their last escape until Mr came home one day with a piece of brass picture chain and two small nuts and bolts. With the aid of the horse man they drilled a hole in the tip of one right and the other ones left horn and the two rams were joined together with the chain with a bolt each end and put in the meadow. The theory was one couldn't climb the hedge bank joined to the other and nowhere was a gap or a gate wide enough for two side by side. When it came to tea time I decided to play the idiot London boy. I said, 'Those rams?' He turned to me and said, 'Yes what about them?' 'Well, when it comes to tupping time, whose job will it be to line the ewes up side by side?' Mrs nearly choked on her tea trying not to laugh. He looked from her to me. I kept an innocent but enquiring face. He looked at her and said, 'I cannot see what's so funny.'

Chapter 34   a bit of a knock

I noticed Bess was letting the foal feed less and less. I told the horseman and he had noticed too and said she's weaning him off. When she was eventually dry she went back in her stall and I started working her again. The pony went, to free the stall for the colt so he could get used to the grooming and wearing bits of harness and to take a bridle with bits in the mouth. I felt much happier now with a routine and the satisfaction of coaxing him to accept the gear and he was growing fast.

A while later during a spell of nice weather two men arrived one carrying a worse-for-wear bag. They smelt like farriers. Mr said put the halter on the colt and take him up the meadow. The two men put a system of rope and pulleys on him and folding his legs under him and laid him on the ground helpless. I asked 'What are you going to do to him?' The horse man, who was holding his head down, said, 'He has got to be castrated.' I felt sick - why couldn't he grow big and powerful like his dad.

I was just thinking, if just one of them mentions doing the other colt which, in their bucolic way they think funny, I will do somebody in injury. Mr shouted at me 'Don't stand there in a dream boy. Run and get the irons from the fire.' I had not been told about the irons before he shouted 'Now boy not next week.' I ran and, poking out of the kitchen fire, were two big soldering irons - which I ran back with. They were glowing red. I gave them to the men. The smell of burning flesh rose up and a flashback had me standing rigid - but Mr was saying 'Where's the lard boy?' which was the first I had heard about lard

- then someone said 'The dog's got it'. By the time I retrieved it there was not a great deal left but it had to do - so it was wrapped around the wounds. They undid the ropes and the, now to be called, gelding got up - but when I went to hold his halter and comfort him he turned away from me and gave a half hearted kick.

It was explained to me that, if left entire, they were dangerous as well as expensive. Mr said he must be kept on his feet for 24 hours. He said he would go out to see him every half hour until one and I could cover until milking time. I asked why? The answer was to stop him going stiff, of course – well, I suppose I should have known that. What I did know was that by being involved I had lost his trust.

Mr said one morning 'We will grade lambs this morning. I have done so well due to the hybrid vigour of course.' I agreed saying, 'Could not be anything else could it?' I got the usual blank look and he went on to say 'I want you to catch any lamb that weighs 70 lbs and bring them to me.' Well you soon learn not to choose too many under the weight. He was finally satisfied with around 20 and he brought them into the market. When he came back from the market Saturday apparently he had plenty of congratulations for getting them to market at least a fortnight early and consequently a higher price than usual. He was so jovial, Mrs said, 'That's nice dear - pity you got rid of the Southdown.' I looked at her - there was a twinkle in her eyes and a small smile at the corner of her mouth. By the time I looked back at her face it was blank.

About the second week in April, when I was on my half day, Mum told me she had an offer of a house on Wood Estate which she would accept. It would knock about two miles off Peter and Dorothy's walk to school and there was a flush water toilet and a tap indoors and so the move was arranged, I said I will get my half day changed, she said, 'No, as soon as you get back, or early tomorrow morning, give him a weeks notice,' I did not ask why ... but wondered 'what about the law.' Mum never did anything without thought so I just rode on back and as luck would have it Mr was in the kitchen so I said, 'I'm giving a weeks notice.' He said, 'You cannot do that.' I thought I was going to get the legal bit but no, he started out, 'You are monthly paid.' I replied, 'Only for your convenience because you have never got seven and six!' and he left me and slammed the door, and his parlour door. I said goodnight to Mrs and went to bed.

Next morning I was just finishing milking when he looked in the shippen but said nothing. When I went into breakfast Mrs looked at me, a bit sadly, I thought. He said nothing until I'd finished – then he said, 'You're running short of hay for the cows.' That was no news to me, I had mentioned it a couple of times before. 'You had better put Bess in the load cart.' I did so, plus two pitchforks and the hay knife, and off we went to the rick, I backed the cart up beside the rick and started cutting out the hay. I stayed on the hay-cart and built up the load using the 'leys' (dialect for the side-bars) for height. When it was full I was standing about ten foot from the ground (above three metres) finishing the load when he, once again, departed from a lifetime's training and instead of the usual 'Stand steady Bess', he said, 'Up Bess,' and she moved forward and, I suppose because of the rocks, the cart jerked sideways and I saw the ground coming to meet me. It seemed to be taking its time - then I hit. I lay there wondering why and started to get up and finally made it.

Mr suggested I go to the house for a cup of tea. I had to stop a few times because deep breaths caused a soreness in my chest. I went in the house and sat at the table not saying a word. I heard Mrs pottering about and a cup of tea was put in front of me. Mr came in and I could hear muted conversation. He said, 'When you feel ready you can do a bit of digging in the garden, it will be easy enough it's sandy soil.'

With the best will in the world I went out and soon found out I could not raise or lower my foot to push the shovel in without pain in my chest so, without telling him, I put the shovel away, retrieved my bike and soon found I could not even ride that. Every time I raised my knees to push down on the pedal there was a click and a stabbing pain in my lower chest - so I set out to walk home pushing the bike.

Just before I reached home Mum met me. Before she asked I said, 'I fell off the hay cart Mum.' She said, 'Right, I will take your bike home. You go to the doctors.' So I went back the way I had come until I met the lane that turns left towards Sticklepath, where I went left again and just over the bridge was Dr Sharps. I went down into his waiting room and found there was no way I could let anyone know I was there. Somehow he became aware and asked me what I was doing there. I said I had fallen off a wagon. His voice matched his name. He said, 'Walk over there,' and pointed into a corner. When I reached there he said, 'Come back here,' then he said, 'Go to Topsham Hospital, Exeter tomorrow,' and he left, so I went home - not far short of an eight mile round trip.

When I reached home again and said what Dr Sharp had said I took my shirt off and low down on the right side of my chest were two blue lumps which were very sore. I got dressed and was told to keep warm. When my brother was coming home from school Mum went to meet him and took him with her to the farm. I was ignorant of what happened there at the time and my brother has only recently told me what transpired. Apparently she knocked on the door and, when Mr opened it, she said she had come for my belongings. Mr said, 'But he will be back.' Mum said, 'No he won't. I am not leaving him here to be ignored.' He replied, 'He cannot give his notice - it's against the law.' Mum countered with 'So what you are going to do about it?' and marched out leaving him spluttering.

Next morning we set out for Topsham, walking to South Zeal to catch the bus for the 20 mile trip. Having got to Exeter we found we needed another bus out to Topsham. The hospital seemed quiet but they were soon two doctors talking to mum as a nurse took me to a cubicle and said get undressed and asked me to put on a sort of loin cloth and then I was x-rayed. Amazing really when you consider that there had been no appointment. Anyway after the x-ray there were three doctors talking to Mum and suddenly she stood up and said, 'How would I know? He was in the care of the medical profession from 18 months to 4 years!' The talk all went soft then and Mum sat down again and explained what had been done at Guy's Hospital London. It seems what they were concerned about was not only the two recent bad greenstick fractures but evidence of many more received at a much earlier age. They finally concluded that most probably it was the strapping down of my torso, while stretching my leg to get the hip back in, that was the cause.

So I was trussed up worse than a turkey and we went home. A few days later a man arrived wanting to see me. I wondered 'What now?' but it seems Mum was expecting him. He knew about the injury and told me to present myself at the farm at 12 o'clock the following Wednesday and I would receive the residue of my wages, plus I was to sign a form for a further 15 shillings which represented the live-out wage compensation because I could not work. The following Wednesday I was right on time, wondering what sort of reception I would get, but they invited me in into the parlour where there was a form to sign plus the money plus a pen and they were all smiles like a jovial old couple. I did the job, received the money, said, 'Thank you,' they saw me out and called goodbye pleasantly, I replied and plodded home puzzled. If only he had been like that from the beginning and he had controlled his temper he would not have lost the equivalent of month's wages (for a horse man) for no gain whatsoever or did they act pleasant so that I might change my mind and come back? I certainly did not know what to expect and Mum was not saying.

During the next week Mum was busy packing things ready for the move to Wood Estate. I helped without too much bending about and Peter manfully re-bagged the coal and a lorry arrived and the move was underway. Mum knew the owner, who had been a friend of the Taylor's at Taw Green Mill, and by bedtime we were fully at home at 2 Wood Cottages. No more digging holes to empty the soil bucket or keeping the pump primed and carrying water - heaven.

On the last week of my sick-leave, when I came in from a reconnoitre of the new territory we were in; there were plenty of moles to be caught, I saw the lorry that shifted us leaving the cottages. It seemed a bit strange because Mum, who would not tolerate debt, would have paid on the nail. The man, who arranged for my payments, came and said I would receive my last payment on Wednesday and would start work the next day. I was shocked and looked at Mum but saw no reaction, and off he went. Dismayed I turned to Mum but she looked happy and then she said, 'You start work on Thursday with Alf Johns - the man that shifted our furniture. It's an eight o'clock start but it would be a good idea to be gone by seven.' I said, 'It will only take ten minutes to get there.' Then I realised, if anyone came looking for me because I had not turned up at the farm, she would send them packing because I was now legally employed elsewhere.

The cottages on Wood Estate
Front - we lived in the middle one

Rear of Wood estate cottages

Chapter 35 a whole new start

So I set out for my new job with a sort of apprehensive feeling of relief at my escape but not knowing what my new job entailed. I soon arrived at my destination and there was his lorry in the drive. The first part of the house was ancient, granite with mullion windows, and going off at right angles was a Georgian house with typical large windows with a front door sitting in the middle. There seemed to be no one around so I went to the door in the old part and called out and was answered by 'come on in'.

Straight in front of me, with the door open, was some sort of storeroom called, as I was told, the backhouse and a short passage to the right at the end of which was a typical old farmhouse kitchen with the usual big fixed table down the side. Mr Johns was sitting at the end and an old lady sitting between it and the wall. He said, 'You're early Frank, sit down and have a bit of breakfast. I don't think we will get moving much before eight-thirty.' I said, 'Thank you but I have had breakfast,' but as though he never heard me he said, 'Mother, cut the boy a slice of bread and put some cream on it - he looks to be built up a bit.' I watched in amazement at the slice she cut - it could have made two full sandwiches. She put jam on the bread, a great dollop of cream on that, then another spoon of jam on top. I could hardly believe it!

There was still something bothering me and I suddenly realised when I had arrived I had heard cows so I asked, 'I heard cows when I arrived?' dreading the reply. 'Mother does the milking, makes the butter and cream.' Alf replied. I heard a disturbance along the passage and Alf said, 'Go and help load the lorry. I will be finished here soon and we will be off.' I went to help the other lad, whose name I have forgotten, but we reloaded the tools. There were a variety of shovels, pick-axes, long saws with a handle each end, ropes, and a crowbar as tall as me. I did wonder what sort of work we were going to do. I had to ride in the back and finally the lorry backed up a rough lane and there was a circular saw bench with an engine, and a big old 6 wheel lorry. The axes and saws were transferred to it and it was driven further up the lane into woodlands past where it had already been cleared. and there were only the fresh stumps left.

Alf said we usually work separately but you will be with me until you can use an axe properly. He then told me we were clearing the land that was a farm abandoned at the turn of the century. British farming was fighting ruin and now was needed to feed the nation and with a bitter tone he said, 'And when this war is over cheap foreign grain will come in again, and our farmers will starve again.' He picked an axe off the lorry and said, 'You bring that one.'

Alf was over 6 foot tall and by the time I picked up the axe he was well away. I had a chance to catch up when he stopped where the trees started. I could hear the other lad's axe ringing and the sound of a falling tree. When I got my breath back I said, 'This axe is worn out and blunt.' He said, 'I know – that's why I call it 'old bumble head' and that is what I'll teach you how with, when you can swing and handle that correctly and accurately I have a new 7lbs (3 kilo) axe for you.'

He went on to show me how to stand and swing an undercut and left me to it. By lunch time I had managed to get a couple of trees down - a bit raggedly. When Alf appeared and said, 'Not bad,' and with a few flicks of his axe neatened up the top of my stumps. As I had lunch I thought 'In one day I have had explanation, instruction and encouragement!' So before lunch was over I took one of the files used to sharpen axes and, as best I could, sharpened bumble head. We worked on until about 3 o'clock, then loaded what had been cut onto the big lorry.

Alf said, 'You carry on here - we will take this load down to the saw bench, when we are finished I will give a couple of blasts on the hooter and you come down and we are off.' After they went I could hear the saw bench. I carried on felling more trees, limbing-out and stacking the branches to burn later. I thought 'What a difference - everything explained. And not a word about London boys not knowing how to swing an axe!' I heard the hooter and went down. The two ton lorry was loaded with logs, all the tools were loaded on top - plus me.

We stopped at a large house and the logs were tipped off. The owner came out and paid. I learnt it was £3 for the two ton and I, for one, went home happy despite the fact that, for some reason, my shoulders were aching.

Over the next few weeks we came to the abandoned farm buildings. The roofs had fallen in and there was a tree growing out of the house - and I got a new axe.

Mum suggested I might join the ATC (air training corps) which met Wednesday evening and learn morse code and navigation and meet some of the local lads. I had already met two girls that lived in the estate and, as Mum put it, who were constantly 'cooeing' from the woods opposite the house.

I joined the ATC, cycling in with two lads from the estate to South Zeal school, slightly older than me and both engineering apprentices - it was hard discussing anything with any of the lads. Our backgrounds were so different and my time at the farm had not helped. I had no small talk and found I could hardly string a sentence together. I had no trouble with the ATC officer. He was a Londoner and I was picking up morse-code and navigation and we started attending the miniature rifle range .22 calibre. I came to realise I had a natural aptitude for shooting.

The other lad working for Alf went into the air force because his girlfriend had joined the WAAFs and he wanted to be with her. I could not see how that would happen, but anyhow I was riding in the cab now and, because the trees were coming into leaf, the operation was moved to woodlands belonging to Fuge Manor. Alf and I loaded the saw bench and fixed a bar in the back of the Ford to the front of the Morris and he said, 'You climb up into the Morris. She's not taxed for the road, so you start following me. When I wave my arm up and down gently, come to a stop with the brake.' I thought, 'Well if you think I can do it – you're the boss - so here goes!' Truth was, I was dwarfed by that cab and the steering wheel was a metre across, but off we went. I had never concentrated so hard in my life. On our way we passed through a few villages but finally arrived. Alf got out, came back and said I had done well. I don't know what he would have said if I had panicked or a policeman had seen it!

The next day Alf drove the Morris down a steep drive into Fuge Bottoms. There had been a lot of huge beech trees at one time but a timber company had felled them and had taken the trunks away leaving the branches and tops. Alf got the lot, for the clearing and taking away, and he said there was no date by which time it had to be cleared so we could drop back to it between his regular contracts, usually on larger farms, so there was a constant change in the type of work.

Alf never seemed to refer to or know anything about my previous job but one day when we were working taking wheat from the thresher to the granary on a large estate Alf said, 'That man you had trouble with before - he's over there.' I said, 'Hang on I'll get a pitchfork.' Then he added, 'and he has his 'little maid' with him.' I looked in amazement. Little maid? She looked like a badly weathered version of him. She was wearing a tattered black jacket and waistcoat, off-white shirt and a skirt to mid calf with the bottom six or eight centimetres coated with what might have been mud, and a big pair of boots with no laces. I just could not believe that her father could harbour such blind delusion as she was a 'little maid' - if she stood upright she would be at least six foot.

To aid my navigation I started using an old North Devon map and a tiny compass, off the top of a pencil sharpener, which I still have. I never drove fast in country lanes as Alf had said if we had a crash we would lose a few days work doing the repairs - but he always drove at 30 miles per hour because that was the law. He'd had an apprenticeship as a mechanic in his youth so all repairs were done at home. He saved spares from engines the same model as his two ton Ford. Most engine spares came from cracked blocks caused because somebody had not drained the cooling system and they were then split by the frost. As a result he had a loft full and when the engine was giving trouble we would replace pistons or their rings, valves, anything needed to have the lorry on the road next morning. So again I was learning something of use to me in the future.

One day we were heading off on a new job and I was working on my navigation and I said, 'Is this job in the middle of Hatherleigh Common because that is where we will be in ten minutes at this speed?' He checked and said, 'I wondered whether your navigation was any good. I don't need navigation - I know where I'm going.' I then realised I was working for a joker at the time.

In the time I was with Alf we worked on many farms where the farm was the same name as the farmers. They were often very interbred and as a result were mentally slow - though fantastic on their own land - and had agents looking after their dealings with authority. One farm, where we took the saw bench to cut their logs for the Winter, the men were small wiry individuals with small beards and they all looked the same. Alf said, 'It's no good trying to count them.' Earlier that year three had received letters to attend medicals prior to call up and none had attended, so the police turned up to take them. They should not have received the letters because none of the men could read. Apparently they showed the police a large printed card, which had their agents and solicitors names and phone numbers on, who soon sorted things out.

At another farm called Palk, Mr and Mrs were quite small but their two sons were massively built and had 'been away' as their mother put it and so they were behind with a ploughing. It was not the first time Alf had been there. Mrs seemed the only one doing the organising. Alf said, 'I will have to leave Frank to do the job - I will start him off.' She said, 'Oh well it won't be the first bit of wobbly ploughing done here,' and went away cackling like an old hen. I said, 'I cannot plough.' 'Now don't worry,' said Alf 'I will do the first 5 rows and you have only to follow them. Just two more things - don't go in for dinner. Mrs will come out and invite you in, and before you ask why, she will treat you like her sons. She will fill your plate as fast as you can empty it and you will have to lay down the rest of the day - and the other thing is, before you go home turn the plough into the next furrow, drop the plough in for about 10 feet, leave it in gear, take the points out of the distributor and put them in your pocket. I will come mid-afternoon tomorrow and we will load the tractor.'

In the morning when I went to the field the tractor was not where I left it but at least 200 metres away against the far hedge. I felt in my pocket for the points. I still had them. I put the points back but I had a job to get between the front and the hedge let alone swing the starting handle. I eventually got a start, made a bit of a mess jolting the plough out of the ground, but eventually got ploughing. By the time Alf came I was finished and waiting. He said, 'Where was it?' I said, 'How did they start it?' He said, 'They did not. They turned the starting handle all the way!' 'But Alf, you said ploughing the ground was equal to one and a half tons and the tractor is about the same, plus the compression of the engine?' He went on to say that many years ago he just left the tractor and in the morning their mother was going mad as her 'boys' had managed to start it, got it in gear and could not get it out nor did they managed to lift the plough out of the ground and just went round and round making a mess, then went out through a gate, without opening it, and drove it home to see if their Mother could stop it and having ploughed through her vegetable garden they finally stalled it. They had shattered the plough shear and the tow bar. 'So now I never leave any engine without immobilizing it.' I did ask why he ever came back and the answer was old Mrs Palk and his mother had been good friends at school when they were young.

Chapter 36   cider, compass and ATC

I gradually began to learn more at the ATC and went with the group to spend a weekend at an RAF fighter station where we had demonstrated how the WAAF straightened out and repacked parachutes, but the most interesting part to me was the almoners workshops where the machine guns were serviced and fitted back in the wings of the hurricanes and spits. On one of these visits we were at dinner when a RAF sergeant and an officer were coming along behind the men eating asking 'Any complaints?' About eight places from me one man said something and the Sergeant ordered him to stand, pick up his dinner and marched him away, so I made up my mind never to complain, just bung on some more salt and get it down!

At the end of the weekend two of us were detailed to fold the blankets and we were told that a wagon would come along and take us and the blankets back to the stores. We folded them all up and a man in RAF uniform came in to collect us. The wagon he drove had rows of big metal bins in the back, and the smell told you what was in them – he was emptying the latrines. It was also splashed all over the truck bed, but he threw the blankets up on to it anyway. When we got to the stores and we started to unload them and take them in, he said to the WAAF lady behind the counter that we had been a lot of wet-the-beds. She gave us a look of disgust - which annoyed me as it was all his fault.

The work with Alf took a hilarious turn. For four weeks now the farmers had been picking the apples to keep. The rest were shook down and gathered up in heaps and we were to take them to Whiteways for cider making commercially, or to cider-making farms for return to their source for use at harvest time. When we went to the farm to pick up the loads, these bruised and fermenting apples (complete with slugs, drunken wasps and much else) were shovelled into sacks, which we carried out on our backs and loaded on the lorry and then we were off. The backs of our shirts were sticky with juice and after an hour against the warm leather seats, apple fumes began to rise and, even with the windows open, by the end of two loads we were both singing. Alf said he thought 'we had better sit in the shade until the lanes stopped wobbling about' quite straight faced. After a while I said, 'How about finishing the job?' He said, 'Sit still, the cream and scones will be here in a minute,' and sure enough the ladies arrived with baskets loaded. I asked how many more farms to do? The answer was five - and tradition must be respected!

I was relieved when that job was finished and we went back to logging. We delivered two ton of logs to a man in Okehampton on our way home one day and just as we had unloaded the tools and were ready the man came out and said, 'How do I know that is two tons? Has it been weighed?' Alf said, 'No.' The man said, 'Well then I want it put on the public weigh-bridge!' Alf said, 'Load the tools.' I thought we would take it to another customer but – no, Alf said, 'Jump up on top Frank. The customer will ride.' The weigh-bridge was down by the cattle market. We took off the tools and drove onto the bridge. Alf took some sacks out of the cab. Alf went over to the office and said to me to start putting logs in the sack, and just as I started on the third sack he shouted, 'Put the last one back on,' paid the operator and showed the customer the ticket, plus a ticket from his wallet which show the lorry's unladen weight from the previous time. He loaded the tools back on, plus the sacks of logs and we went back to the customers place, took off the sacks and tools and tipped. I noticed Alf had backed close to his woodshed door, which meant he would have to move them before he could get the door open. We reloaded the tools and the sacks of logs and he came out with the money, looked at the sacks and said, 'Aren't they are part of my load?' Alf took the money and said, 'They would have been, sir, and I thank you for saving me from breaking the law. It's just as illegal to give overweight as it is underweight,' and left him spluttering.

On the way home Alf called at a cottage and an old lady came to the door. He took the sacks and tipped the logs out and said, 'There's some logs for you mother.' She said, 'I haven't the money for them.' He said, 'They are already paid for mother - by a kind man in Okehampton.' On the way home he explained if he had just driven off, the word would have gone round - that he had left the scene because he knew the load was underweight; however by meeting the challenge and then thanking the customer for saving him from breaking the law by giving too much, the customer could not say he stopped himself from being cheated. In the meantime, from the weighbridge operator, nearly everybody would know the customer had 'robbed' *himself* of nearly 5 kilos of logs.

On a further ATC visit to a fighter station we were taken to a domed building where the art of air-gunning was explained how to aim according to the range and angle of flight whether it was climbing or diving. In the centre of the dome was a gunners seat with a sight, which was concentric rings the same as a tail gunner in a bomber. We were shown the controls that swung the seat where you wanted. Then the lights in the dome went out and projected on the inside of the dome was a German fighter diving at an angle across my front. I caught it in my front sight laid off for the speed and pushed the button trigger. As it hits, you receive the sound of it exploding in your headphones and immediately another one is diving at you and then a third, each one at a different altitude and speed. I hit all three and I knew I had found my forte and now I knew what I wanted to do. Naïve madness certainly!

The Germans were attacking Plymouth at this time and on our way back from the RAF station we had dropped off the Okehampton lads and I arrived at South Zeal in the dark. We were met by the village policeman, Mr Lytton, with half a dozen special constables - all of whom were moor farmers. Apparently someone was lighting fires beyond Cheriton Coombe and we three were to go with them to put out the fires - which were not large because the heather and gorse was damp. After a long stumbling journey we arrived at the first fire and had to resort to breaking of gorse branches with our bare hands to beat out the fire and then stumbled onto the next and so on and still we could see new ones flare up.

One of the Moor men said, 'He is using paraffin I can smell it. He will run out soon,' and after another six or so he sneaked away. Of course, in the pitch black we could not see him but, because he saw his fires going out, he probably knew we were catching up.

Mr Lytton said, 'The problem now is - where are we? Do any of you Moor men know?' There was silence. He went on to say, 'I thought so. Well it's too late to see where the sun went down and too early to see any indication where it will come up in the east so my next question is, have any of you gentleman got a compass?' Still more silence so risking being thought to be an idiot I said, 'I have,' and he said with slight annoyance in his voice, 'Let me have it then!' and held out his hand. I said, 'Be careful, it's rather small,' and put it in the palm of his hand and he said, 'My God it's no bigger than a sixpence! Follow me gentleman, north, northwest by this little gem and we should hit the Rowley Road, turn left then and South Zeal.' We followed him stumbling along in the pitch black and found the road. When we reached South Zeal he said, 'Before you go gentleman I will shine my torch and you may have a look at what has just brought you back to your warm beds for the night,' and showed them my small compass. I still have it. *(see photo)*

By the time I made it home it was past two. Because Mum's younger sister Daisy and young son had come to stay a while I was sleeping on the sofa in the living room and so disturbed nobody and was gone in the morning before they were up. When I returned in the evening Mum said, 'I'm afraid your shoes are badly singed. You might get some polish on them but the bottoms of your uniform trousers are beyond doing anything with. I expect they will change them,' but she did not ask how it happened and I thought she would find out through the usual sources.

As the year went on the work with Alf constantly changed. One day, when towing the old Morris, with me behind the wheel, as we were passing a place where a fir plantation was being felled, Alf waved me down and stopped and got out and stood talking, I surmised, about any deciduous wood to clear up. I looked to my left and there was a beautiful timber girl with a billhook that was much too heavy for her so I got down and climbed the hedgerow bank and went to where she was. My chat up line was, 'May I show you how to do that Miss?' and she let me show her how to cut the branches in line with their growth and started to make progress and chatting away soon knew her name. I was just about to ask if I could meet her somewhere when they were shouts from the men on the road. Alf had got back in his cab and started the engine. I simply flew over the fallen tree trunks over the bank, sprinted to the Morris, scrambled in and just removed the handbrake as the tow tightened and we were off. We arrived at our new location and parked the Morris and Alf never said a word just as though he was not aware that I was not in the cab and I was not going to ask. He probably was aware and that was just the sort of joke he would pull. Needless to say I never saw the girl again. I began to realise that even with an employer like Alf, who would talk about all sorts of subjects, I was still not making contact with anyone my own age and those I knew in the ATC had nothing in common, their background and outlook was totally at odds with mine.

One instance being; a German bomber, turning over South Tawton and Taw Green as they often did when bombing Plymouth which is only 30 miles away across the moor, decided to get rid of what he had got left - I think it was five bombs, and no bigger than 125 kilos each. You could jump across the craters, none of which was near any house or farm by at least 400 metres, and they never even woke up anyone. Everybody was saying they had been bombed and how frightening it was. I could only think, 'They don't know what is happening to people in Plymouth. They have not felt the concussion up through their feet or the smell of burning and I hope they don't,' but I could, and it stayed locked up in my own head.

We continued our visits to air stations and whenever there was a chance of a session in the dome I was there. When we made these visits we were told to bring a note from a parent agreeing if we wanted a flight, usually in the station commander's personal bi-plane - a Miles Magisters. I struck lucky one time and was duly 'fitted' with a parachute. I think it was fitted, though it was dragging against the back of my heels. The pilot said a few confidence-building words such as 'Make sure you know where the ripcord is, keep a check on the takeoff and airspeed - the gauge is on the wing'. Sure enough on the wing strap was a quadrant-shaped piece of tin with a spring attached carrying a six centimetre square of tin. When the forward speed of the plane pushed the gauge to 270 kilometres the plane could take off. Next he said that 'When there was complete cloud cover like today we may be up there waiting to dive on anyone taking off, so keep your eyes on the cloud. If one comes I will try to gain enough height to turn over and tip you out.' Well by the time you watched the gauge and the clouds, we were landing again and we climbed out. He said, 'Did you enjoy that?' I thought nuts to you so I said, 'It was disappointing Sir.' Instead of leaving it he said, 'And why is that?' I said, 'There was no Messerschmitt.'

My 'little gem' of a compass that got us off the Moor that night

Chapter 37   shooting, scythe and Yanks

Autumn was doing its usual stint of leaf drop so it was back to clearing farmland and as usual we worked apart, working around trees too large to fell alone, and at lunchtime would arrange to take them down with the long saw - which was 11 foot (3 and a half metres) long. To use this saw two people knelt each side of the tree with their backs to the direction it was to fall then, staying up on their knees and leaning forward they take a light grip of the handle at their end and, remembering to only pull, start to saw - soon a rhythm is achieved. As the cut moves towards you, without losing the rhythm, you would have to shuffle back. If Alf thought you were losing the rhythm, by watching the progress of the teeth through the trunk, he would throw his dentures down in front of you and say 'If you want to watch teeth, watch those!' When the tree begins to fall you remove the saw, stand and move back and away at an angle from the stump. The reason for this is that when the head of the tree hits the ground it can come straight back or kick off at any angle and deliver a bone-breaking thump.

From time to time the customer of the load of logs required it splitting, so I would put my bike up on the load and when the load was tipped at the customer's I would stay behind, split the logs to the customers approval, tie the axe on my bike and cycle home with half a crown (two shillings and six-pence) That much would have bought seven large loaves and six penny pastries - as an example.

The target-shooting on the small range of Zeal Head carried on. I had acquired a point 22 garden-gun which was built like a rifle except the bore was smooth for fine shot, but was reasonably accurate with solid bullets up to around 20 metres and, with some careful stalking, could take a rabbit - which equalled four shillings profit to me. By volunteering to issue the rounds per shooter at Zeal Head a few always found their way into my pocket.

One day it was suggested that a 'thru'penny' (3d) sweep would make the shooting more interesting. Evening by evening the number of participants increased; all the special constables, even the village copper and his wife joined in. I had still not fully realised my natural ability to shoot when, on one particular evening, it transpired that I had tied for top score with a 'special' called Ian, and there was a buzz of interest as a 'sudden death' shoot off was called for - one shot each. I hadn't realised that the build-up of interest was purely to find someone to beat the London boy.

They decided to do the shoot-off standing, as 'Ian be good at shooting standing with a shotgun'. Ian went first. When the card was brought back he had clipped the edge of the bull - it was duly admired with exclamations of, 'You've beat him for sure!' I was then handed my bullet. In an atmosphere of 'why is he bothering, the competition is over' I took my shot, standing, and when someone went down for the card he walked back looking at it. When he reached us, without a word, he held it up - there was a gasp! Someone said, 'He be further into the bull than Ian.' I turned to Ian - he already had the winnings in his hand and without a word he put them in mine. There was not a word of congratulations from anybody. So, because of my newfound skill, I pocketed the winnings that night, the equivalent of a quarter of a week's wages for a farm hand.

After that the attendance at the range dwindled down to just Home Guard and ATC again. A Home Guard officer invited the ATC to visit the full-bore range (303) at Quarry Hills where they had a range where they practiced once a month. The rifles were Canadian Ross and, with the butt on the ground, were nearly as tall as me and with the bayonet fitted, made us look ridiculous, but when it was our turn to shoot I, and another lad, John Mallett, put up scores that impressed the officers who asked how old we were, and when we said they told us, 'When you are 17 we would like you to join the Home-Guard.' Personally I wished I was 17 already to have one of those rifles.

We had started to learn morse code at the ATC and proceeded to aldis lamps to practice at night with but always with informing the local observer corps of our intentions on time of operating beforehand. One night we were operating from Ramsley Common across the valley to a moorland field on Cheriton Combe, in the dark I saw, using a pair of old Paris opera glasses that had better night vision than the average binoculars, movement in the field to the left. I flashed the message "Ominous movement adjacent to the left". About halfway through their reply of "message not understood" they were suddenly surrounded by the Home Guard from Throwleigh who had been alerted by an Observer Corp at

Okehampton - who had not received the warning of our intentions to practice. Of course there was an inquiry but the Observer Corp was congratulated on their alertness and of course 'that London boy had caused the problem by using words not commonly used in the local vernacular'. I thought 'so much for the rule of brief and precise then'.

We were issued with two no 5 send-and-receive radio sets. The number 5 denotes a range. The Home Guard soon recognised their usefulness and included us. One night, when practicing, a strange voice broke in asking who we were and we replied ATC. Then voice said, 'Why are you on this wavelength?' We replied that the sets were as we received them. He then asked where we were. We said, 'South Zeal' and after a few minutes he came back saying 'My navigator tells me you're almost eleven miles from us. We are a bomber crew in training. It has been interesting listening but shut down now and get those sets returned. They are interfering with our incoming orders. Out.' So we switched off and the ATC had them returned.

One morning Alf said he would be gone for the day to put in an offer for oak tree tops, the trees having been felled by someone else for the trunks to be sawn into planks for ship decks. As a nation we were running out of ships and all the ship repair yards were fitting ships that had been idle for years. The average 200 year old oak yielded 10 to 15 tons and the bark was needed for the leather industry for the millions of army boots now needed, so Alf said I was to spend the day cutting the banks of nettles in the orchard. I said I was used to this, with a sigh, as I had done scythe work before. 'Just slow easy swings not taking too much time. The scythe is new so don't break it,' Alf added, and off he went.

I started easy swings, point up and got on very well and then, on a backwards swing, the blade came off and was swinging on the wire that runs from the back of the blade to a point about 30 millimetres up the shaft, its job is to sweep the cut material to the left. Alf's new scythe was broken! So I got the bill-hook and carried on cutting the hedge instead. While I was having lunch Alf came back and there on the table was Alf's new scythe. When he saw it he said, 'Have you any money?' I said, 'Yes,' thinking 'but not enough to buy a new scythe'. Alf said, 'When you have finished take it up to the blacksmith and get it mended.'

The blacksmith-shop was on the brow of the hill on the left as you entered South Tawton. I asked him to mend it. He gave one look and said I will fire weld and rivet it this time but that's absolutely the last time! I paid the one shilling and sixpence and took it back, laid it on the table and said, 'The blacksmith told me he cannot mend it again as that was the second time.' Alf picked up the scythe and went out the door. I followed to the door - he was running down his meadow, he jumped the stream and ran up the opposite hill to a farmhouse. The farmer was called Darch and they had two sons bigger than Alf but a bit slow due, I am told, to inbreeding, and I could hear Alf roaring at them. I asked Alf's mum 'Why is he shouting?' She said, 'Old farmer be deafer than a stone.' Alf came back, minus the scythe, and gave me 3 shillings for my trouble - he had sold the scythe to the Darches – the only people who had previously borrowed his new scythe!

A group of us ATC lads started to attend lessons at Okehampton school one evening a week mainly on navigation. Rather than walk our bikes up the very steep hill out of town we used to wait for a lorry struggling up the hill, ride out and catch hold with one hand and get a tow, letting go when we heard him change up at the top.

The ATC officers arranged for a social evening at the school. I told our officer that I would not attend as I could not stand party games and I cannot dance, I have no sense of rhythm probably stemming from my early crippled state. Nevertheless he insisted. He had laid on transport with the owner of Days Garage, Sticklepath who ran a taxi service, to take us and bring us back. Oh well. And it was just as I predicted - there were some very good looking girls there and both them and the lads were wearing immaculately clean and pressed uniforms and were obviously sophisticated town-grammar-school-confident and well used to social gatherings. About halfway through the evening eight black Americans in fatigue dress arrived and they were introduced as a spiritual singing group. I listened with amazement at this beautiful sound they were making - it completely wiped out my initial misery. When they finally finished there was some polite clapping and before the senior ATC officer finished thanking them, the party game started again.

I went to the officer that was with them, who was a much lighter shade of black, and said, 'Would your men like any refreshments. I am sorry we have nothing stronger, because we are underage it's only fruit punch with cinnamon and ginger.' He said, 'Thanks, I'm sure they would.' So I went and got a tray loaded with glasses of punch and carried it to them. When I offered it to them their eyes went wide open and they hesitated and looked over at their officer - he must have given them a nod as they then accepted a glass. I took the tray to the officer last and said, 'No disrespect sir, but they have been singing. I thought for a moment that they did not want the punch.' He said, 'They are enjoying the drink but never before has a white person served them anything.'

I did ask if they sang anything just for fun. He spoke to them and with big grins they started a song accompanied with a movement like sweeping something away across the floor every so often. When they stopped I went forward and thanked them. Suddenly there was enthusiastic clapping from behind me - the singing had stopped their parlour games. I didn't care. Both I and the singers had shared a unique experience. Sometime later I saw part of an old American film with the comedian Costello, of the duo Abbott and Costello, and he was singing doing the same routine as the black spiritual singers and the song was about the Mississippi flooding their cabins and pleading with it to stay away.

Chapter 38   toothache, enemies and dances

The work I was previously doing changed because one of the farms we had cleared was going into production and needed a stone road in and Alf got the contract to supply and deliver the stone. The stone was to be quarried from the tailings from Ramsley Common copper mine that closed over a hundred years ago. The chimney still stands today. The waste stone from the mine had been tipped over the side of the common towards the Throwleigh Road and over the years had weathered and stuck itself together, an aptitude that made it useful for farm roads as it soon sets to a hard-wearing surface.

So my job now was to dig it down, but the hard work was to swing the shovel full out, so that it fell without scattering, to a lower level so it could be shovelled up and thrown down into the lorry at a lower level still - two tons in a load. We did weigh a shovelful once - at 25 pounds, around 12 kilos. We were doing 3 loads a day, 5 days a week. You can imagine the physique I developed. I must admit that if I was not already reasonably strong, through heaving and carrying timber and axe work, I probably would not have lasted the job out the three weeks it took.

In the beginning of the second week I developed a raging toothache and went to a small shop in Ramsley and bought some aspirin and an hour later went again - but she refused to sell me more. I asked where a dentist could be found and she told me number 10 Station Road so I scrawled a note for Alf on the shovel and pedaled off to Okehampton. It was nine miles and when I arrived at No. 10 I knocked and the door was opened by big, beautiful maid with a black dress and a crisp white apron and white cap on her head. I asked to see the dentist. She asked if I had an appointment. I replied that it was an emergency. She said to wait and disappeared shutting the door and came back to say, come back at twelve; so I went into the park and sat down on the grass, right opposite the house, and watched the door

I never saw anybody arrive or leave but come twelve I knocked on the door again and was shown into a front room on the right, empty, except for a big chair with arms, which was not a usual dentist chair. I thought perhaps it was only a waiting room but after a while the dentist came in. He was big, must have been towards 20 stone. He did have a white coat on. I showed him which tooth. A molar second from the back left lower jaw. He looked, grunted a bit and his breath hit me like pub chucking-out time. He hauled a pair of forceps out of his pocket, gripped the tooth and did a straight lift upwards. I came up out of the chair. He bellowed 'Sit down you coward!' and as he lowered his arm I fastened my arms under the chair and had another go. This time he almost got the chair off the floor but the tooth came out and as it did so the pliers cracked against my top teeth - and then he went out. No offer of a rinse – nowhere to spit it out. The maid appeared and held out her hand for seven shillings and sixpence. That would have been a third of a farm workers weekly wage! (I recently had a tooth removed in a modern dentist for £11 under the NHS It is now 2012 and at the minimum wage of £5/hr the extraction was worth just over 2 hours work. I think we were right to lobby for a health service at the end of the war.)

I went to the shop in Ramsley and bought a packet of salt, went back on the job, poured the salt in the last of the cold tea I had, rinsed my mouth and carried on digging out the next load. When Alf arrived we loaded the lorry. He never referred to my absence and my pay was the same as usual.

The road where the stone was being taken was being laid by Italian prisoners of war, wearing British battledress with big yellow patches in the back and on the trousers - I thought that was just about right. One day at lunchtime Alf brought four of them, supposedly, to help me. What a waste of time that was. There was not one of them could lift a full shovel of stone and the tiny amount they could lift they scattered down the bank – useless. I told Alf 'You have to take them away.' He said they could rake it down and then they watched us load the lorry. I formed the opinion that they were suffering from the Mediterranean syndrome (idleness). Alf left so by the time four of them fiddled about digging some stone down I was fuming - I was not going to get a load in time for Alf's return. While I was shovelling stone down to the next level they sloped off. I would have seen them had they passed on the road so they must have gone to my left where there was a valley leading up to Ramsley Common. I did not know what my responsibility was regarding them but the mere fact that they disregarded me meant I lost my temper. I knocked the head off my pickaxe and, taking the shaft, I went straight up the face of the tailings and there they were gazing around on the Common. I ran straight at them. The look of shock on their faces - I don't think they could understand how I came up the quarry face. I left them in no doubt that their mothers did not know their fathers and drove them back on the job.

Needless to say when Alf arrived I had a full load and before he said anything, knowing one knew English, I told him not to bring them near me again. I said, 'I'll end up getting hung for killing one. I'd sooner volunteer so I could kill the useless sods legitimately.' As usual he said nothing but he took them away. The second, and last, load Alf said 'Job finished. Put your bike on. We will have lunch when we get there,' meaning 'on the job' after we tipped the last load. Before we started lunch we went to the farm house for a cup of tea. The Italians were there cooking lunch over an open fire. The army guard was eating his tired-looking sandwiches, rifle hanging on his shoulder and the Italians were gathered round a big frying pan cooking up a heap of bacon and tomatoes and there was enough bread for a company of infantry. Alf tapped me on the shoulder and said, 'Come away before you kick the lot over.' Funny, I was unaware Alf was a mind reader.

Then it was back to Fuge Manor, having nothing to lose my temper over, making my own decisions and producing the logs. One morning an old man arrived and asked Alf to supply him with a load of logs and he went on to say that high ranking German officers had stayed at Fuge Manor in the past, Goebbels, Hitler's propaganda minister to name one.

As we cleared the timber each side of the road it was getting difficult to carry the larger sticks to the wagon, especially on the lower side of the road. I suggested bringing in the tractor. Alf said it could roll over down there. I thought about it and said we could keep it on the road. I'd run a long cable from the tractor to the log and draw them up. He did not seem to go for that but when we headed home we called in at the old chap's farm. I stayed in the cab, I thought he was collecting the price of the logs, and then we went home. Next morning when we arrived the farmer was there holding a great Clydesdale gelding and a roll of cable. I would have liked to work that monster, but every time Alf or I went anywhere near him he stamped one great forefoot, but over the next three days, with Alf and me clearing scrub out of the way and lopping extraneous branches flush to the trunks, all the larger sticks were in a position easily available to us. 'That has done the old boy a bit of good and quietened him down,' the old chap said, and us too I thought. The leaves were coming off so that meant back to clearing farmland.

I was still studying navigation and morse with the ATC and shooting with the Home Guard and sending off mole and rabbit skins. At a meeting one night they suggested putting on a dance in the victory hall, South Zeal, only charging enough to pay for the hall. I was not keen on the idea as the hall is not large and those days there were a lot of American GI's about plus a British army engineering battalion - with not much rapport between them - and worst of all it was proposed to use a gramophone for the music. I did not want to be there, but duty called. The place was nearly too full for dancing with both sorts of squaddies plus there were not many girls, because the farm girls were not into that sort of socialising. Then the group musicians arrived from the engineers, turned off the gramophone and started to play old fashioned dance music. The GI's started to heckle saying trust the British to be behind the times but the group continued to play waltzes with perfectly straight faces and the GI's started to leave and then the music gradually changed to more livelier tunes but when some GI's tried to come back the doorway was blocked by British squaddies jammed in the doorway. I said to our officers 'I think we went some way to improving the goodwill among the allies and I am off home.' And the idiot said 'Do you think so?'

I went home thinking they don't recognise sarcasm either, so I was not best pleased when the Okehampton lot decided to run a dance in the hall too. The hall was half way along the main road on the left and it was two or three steps from the pavement. Again I was prevailed upon to attend and our officer had laid on transport to take us and bring us back. A group of musicians were hired to play this time - I remember one chap had clubbed feet. When we arrived the dancing was in full swing and as I came in I noticed a pair of ATC lads sitting behind a card table taking the entry fees and they actually had the takings lined up on the table a pile of each denomination. As I was not interested in the dancing I said if they liked I would keep an eye on the door and take the fees but they refused so I advised them to keep the cash out of sight and then I got it - they soon told me this was not London. I did think to say when all the troops come off duty they won't be only Devon boys - but said nothing. Apart from getting myself a drink I stood in the foyer.

Much later in the evening when most people were in, a British squaddie was wandering down the opposite pavement and his attention was caught by the music and the lights. I have to say the blackout was not very well observed. Anyway, he started to cross the road. He was quite elderly, possibly permanent staff from the artillery camp, but when he saw me a strange thing happened - he suddenly became slightly inebriated and as he came up the stairs he had to hold on as he passed me. He gave a salute and slightly staggered to the table, forage cap in hand, which he put on the table to stop from falling over. He slurred out 'How much you going to charge a poor old soldier?' when they said 'two shillings.' He said 'I shall have to clear off then,' pulled himself upright and turned towards the door. I had watched the whole charade in fascination and the lads at the table hadn't noticed a thing, so I struck at the cap, which broke his grip on it and half crowns and florins rained down on the floor. He immediately became sober. He called me a 'stinking local' whereupon I spoke for the first time, my accent was pure East End 'Stay North of the Elephant!' As he was going out the door past me he tried a backhanded slap. I pushed his shoulder and he went down the stairs and went round the corner giving pitiful moans. One of the lads from the table came over and said 'He's hurt. Go and see if he is alright.' I said 'You go if you like. He is only trying to get me to go down straight onto his right fist.' I started to tell them what naive idiot yokels they were keeping the cash on the table and how he would have apologized and left taking around two pounds with him - and by the time they'd start wondering where the money was he would have been long gone. Then they amazed me by asking if I knew him, and asked, 'What was all that about elephants?' Then it dawned on me that I had recognised his accent as North London and I had automatically told him to stay out of the East End. The Elephant and Castle pub was the recognised boundary marker. Not a word of which they understood - but I noticed the money was not on show anymore.

Chapter 39 a prediction, a rabbit and arsenic

As it was a rather warm humid autumn, on the way home one day we stopped outside an old country pub and went and sat in the shade at an old table. There was an elderly gypsy lady nearby and, sitting under a tree a bit away, were two old men. Alf said, 'Weather is a bit warm, mother.' The sweat was running off Alf's bald head and dripping off the long fringe onto his shoulders but the old lady said, 'Your boy don't sweat master?' Alf said, 'No mother. It don't matter how hot it gets or how hard he works.' Looking at me she said, 'Young colt that don't sweat more, after doesn't make old bones.' Well I'm glad to say that prediction was wrong as I am now 90. I finally did break out in a sweat at least 20 years later in circumstances I will relate in its place in my story.

I have not mentioned it before but Alf was a widower with young daughter and when his old mother died he remarried again. The lady lived in Belstone and it is true to say Alf was now being better organised and the lunch he was bringing to work improved. It had been getting pretty bad as his mother became infirm. On at least one occasion I shared mine because his mother had put in some chicken casserole in a bowl with a piece of rag tied over it and a slice of bread. When he got the rag off, the maggots raced one another to get out! So I shared my egg and bacon flan. Even his young daughter was cleaner and better dressed. One day Alf's wife called me. I said, 'What do you need Rose?' always willing to help but the first thing she said was, 'To you I am Mrs John - and I want you to tell me if Mr John ever buys any tobacco and I do not want you to encourage him to stop on the way home for a pint of beer.' Well - the ignorance of the lady - I mean London Boys don't even grass on their enemies let alone their boss. So I just said, 'Yes Rose.' Funny, we never seemed to get on after that. Typical of what she tried was - getting me to feed the chickens. In the mornings I was always early and loaded the lorry so we could be on our way but then she asked me in the evenings, before I left - sometimes even when I was behind time. So I adopted a rule that I used the rest of my working life. If anybody lumbered me with a job above and beyond my duty I never got it right first. She moaned about the amount of grain left on the ground after the birds had gone to roost ... so I gave them a lot less ... and the next thing the eggs began to diminish because they were not getting enough. She soon stopped trying it on.

That autumn she had persuaded Alf it will be a good idea to store some apples for use through the winter. The trees had not been picked for many years or pruned so were not easy to pick from. Alf borrowed a special ladder for the job. These ladders were about a metre and a half wide at the bottom to stop them tipping sideways and around 6 metres tall and, in use, were laid gently against the twigs outside of the tree, i.e. not against a solid branch and when climbed with a basket were a daunting prospect let alone carrying a full basket down. Things were going alright and she was under the tree happily packing the picked apples into trays when suddenly the ladder tipped sideways and, as I desperately clung on, several apples left the basket and hit Rose. She jumped up and went indoors. After the ladder was righted I carried on picking until it was time to go home. Next morning the full crate had been carried in. Rose had a bruise on her face and, typically, Alf said nothing.

Having joined the Home Guard I was disappointed to receive a sten gun (cheaply made short-barrelled machine gun) instead of a rifle – which I could have used for sniping. I started carrying it to work, after all I worked remote and you never knew where a Jerry may bail out. Their bombers were often about and, I know it probably sounds stupid now, but you needed to live in those times to understand, I took to patrolling the lane that runs from Taw Green to Sticklepath and would peep around the corner and watch the special constables in a group at 'Lady well' and then work my way back home.

On my way out I would set a snare or two and one night, having caught a rabbit, I gutted it and hung it on my handle bars. I was coasting along in the pitch dark, steering by the light where the trees don't quite meet over the road, when the bike came to a sudden stop and I flew over the handlebars and hit the road and rolled, knocking skin off various places. I thought paratroops had landed and put a tripwire across the road. I had heard my sten sliding along the road and, because they are notorious for starting to fire spontaneously, rolled in the ditch and waited for the sound of boots coming - but nothing. I crept along, found the sten gun and when I picked up the bike I found that the rabbit had jammed between the fork and the wheel! I had to hack it off to get my bike to move.

By now the various grazes were making themselves felt and I had at least a mile to go home. When I got there I let myself in and got stripped off and was bathing the damaged skin when the kitchen door opened and Mum stood there looking at the damage. I said, 'I caught a rabbit Mum.' And just as she was closing the door she said, 'Do you think you got that the right way round?' Whether my mother was aware of what I did at night I do not know but I wouldn't be surprised - she was 'fey' (psychic) where I was concerned.

The girl that lived on the estate, whom I used to talk mainly about local happenings, left school at fourteen and went to work for Doctor Sharp in Sticklepath as a home help for Mrs Sharp. Mum lost no time in telling me 'Now you know her age!' I said, 'Mum I have always been aware despite her development by her childish chatter about local families and scandals so don't worry on that score.' She seemed relieved.

Around this time there was a lot more aircraft about and twice we saw badly damaged super fortresses returning from raids over Germany heading for an emergency landing field in North Devon. I suppose being in the ATC we knew a bit more of the development of the various military aircraft and there had been an appeal for silk stockings to plait into glider tow ropes so that a bomber could deliver fully equipped men to any war zone. But I was truly amazed when I was with a group of Home Guards and a bomber passed over towing a glider and one of them said, 'See that one's broken down and that one's towing it home.' I turned to look at their faces. All were straight with a few sage nods, I thought, they still don't get it. I sincerely hope we do not get invaded. They still do not realise what we were up against. I felt that if I knew something they didn't know would it be wrong to enlighten them. As the posters say 'don't crow about what you know about'. I did mention to Alf about the fact they seemed ignorant about the situation the country was in and he said that the world was contained within their farm and Okehampton market and the price of a product.

There seemed to be more military activity; for instance there were soldiers driving Fordson tractors that had been converted into dumpers by seating the driver on the fuel tank with the tipping dumper over the back wheels so that meant the Fordson was being driven backwards i.e. it was steering on the back wheels which meant to go left the steering wheel was turned to the right. Needless to say there were many mistakes and spills. What they were for - remains a military secret as far as I am concerned. Also an American Mobile laundry unit arrived and the black troops manning it were billeted in tents in the field behind the police house at Zeal Head and there were always GI's in South Zeal, where they came from I have no idea.

Alf said they were prospecting for girls, one or two found a welcome at Ramsley - to their cost. The row of cottages, with their backs to Ramsley Common had wells for their water supply but, because they were below the mine, these were contaminated by arsenic - which is also mined with copper. The inhabitants were not affected by the arsenic because they had imbibed it in their mother's milk - but it treated the GI's badly. It is true to say the girls had beautiful complexions.

As time went on there were a lot more GI's about with convoys of the largest lorries ever seen and always on the move. We carried on clearing wood from farmland but now as we worked we were often surrounded by GI's on manoeuvres and they would go by and disappear just like they never saw us. Alf said if they are here to stop us being invaded they should be further east. Nobody will try and land on this coast.

Dad was coming down to see us a bit more often as the raids were dying down. Also there seemed a lot fewer Yanks around and, as winter approached, a lady started to do fish and chips on Friday evenings from a cottage around 30 yards down from the Oxenham Arms. If the fish arrived on the bus from Exeter - sometimes after an anxious wait - I used to have a feed. I would ask her to keep four portions for me to take home to the family and there was opportunity for a bit of socializing with some older girls. When I say older, I mean at least three years older than me. It was good to talk to someone more sophisticated, but when they talked about going to dances ... even if I could dance - I still had no decent clothes.

Chapter 40 barrier, haircut
- and the letter

Christmas came and went and then it was 1944 - the year I would become eighteen – but not until June. The clearing of land became more urgent and our days were spent in increasingly remote places with even less contact socially, except when I went to the Home Guard or ATC.

There was a group from Wood Estate at the ATC and on our way home we used to call in at the Seven Stars in South Tawton. On leaving, on our bikes, having had a few half pints of cider, we'd free-wheel down, as it was fairly steep downhill past the last row of cottages. It being late and dark, some of the lads would yodel and shout. Just past the cottages the road levelled out and, because it was prone to flooding, there was a high walkway on the nearside and the Home Guard had built a barrier draped with barbed wire that could be swung out to block the road.

I was always last away because I could not mount the bike on the move so, when we left the pub one particular night and, as usual, they made the same racket, I was, perhaps, ten metres behind. All of a sudden there was the sound of loud pops and squeals as they ploughed into the barrier that someone has swung across the road, probably to stop the shouting, but thankfully, because I was behind, I was able to stop. The other lads were in a mess. Two had to be carefully extracted, their bikes were embedded, their arms and thighs were lacerated, all front tyres punctured, one completely ruined - and they were not easy to come by. Finally, all were extracted and made their painful way home. Thereafter they went silently and slowly into that dark section of road. Why did they not see the barrier? Well because of the blackout bike lights hardly reached beyond your front wheel but were just enough for anybody to see you coming!

As the year wore on we were so busy that both Alf and I did not find time for a haircut nor did we give it much thought and my tight curly hair had grown into a huge mop, what would nowadays be called an 'afro' style, however mine incorporated bits of wood, lichen and moss, whereas Alf's hair, what he had of it considering he was bald on top, swept his shoulders. So when I received a letter to attend a medical, in mid May in Exeter, we decided to go to the barbers. We headed for the first one on the main street in Okehampton, and as Alf pulled up outside we could see the proprietor standing looking out the window, before we had fully got out of the car he was shooting the bolts and waving us away. He didn't seem to want our custom.

The next barber was the same, he told us to go away – I wonder why? A man nearby the second place told us the only place we'd get a haircut was up by the railway station – so that's where we went. This barber laughed and said he'd do the job as it wasn't the worst he'd tackled. He then showed us a picture of a man, of whom you could only see his eyes and tip of his nose, so much hair and beard did he have. He told us that when it was all cut off he turned out to be a young man of twenty-seven under it all.

Now, all my hair had been protecting my forehead, ears and sides of my face from the weather and sun, and all of a sudden you could see my whole face, that is a small brown face surrounded by a wide pale white rim! Not a good look!

When I went to the medical I had no trouble passing in every particular including my heart, I mention that separately as it will feature much later in my life-story. I began to see myself in that rear-gunners seat and then the examining officer asked me were there any other conditions including childhood illnesses. So I replied that I had spent nearly two and a half years in hospital as a child and my parents had said I had caught just about everything at that time which, as I said, was perfectly par for the course. But he wanted to know why I was there in the first place. So now I was stumped for an answer. Do I say and make light of it. If I tell the truth I might lose my chance for revenge - mad as that sounds. On the other hand if I don't admit it, and it lets me down in, or at any critical time, I might be putting other men in jeopardy. So I said about the congenital hip displacement and the subsequent correction and I added that I have spent the last three years in hard physical labour with no problems. He did not comment so I got dressed.

I had gone to the medical in my ATC uniform because I still did not have any decent clothes. Then an RAF recruiting officer made an appearance and asked if I was volunteering. I said, 'No, I have family commitments to settle first. I must wait for my call up.' Then it became confusing because he said, 'But you're ATC and you will be called up into the army. What have you been doing in the ATC?' I told him radio and navigation and I had found I had an aptitude for air to air gunning and wanted to be a tail gunner, then he wanted to know details of my education (which was chaotic to say the least) then he said I would not make air crew unless I had at least been to grammar school but he said there were plenty of other jobs in the RAF, and I suddenly got a flashback to that latrine wagon and the RAF man emptying all those buckets, and I said, 'No thank you Sir. I'll wait for my call up.' He just disappeared into his office. He was possibly thinking 'what a little idiot', and me thinking 'what do they want an education for to sit in the tail of a bomber'. So I climbed back on the bus depressed and defeated for the journey home.

Sometime later a letter arrived with a card inside declaring me as B2. Now it was more visions of cleaning latrines or perhaps the cook house in the Army. My depression must have got through to Alf because one day out of the blue he said, 'You don't have to go. I can get you deferment for war work.' I said, 'No thanks Alf.' I think Mum may have had a hand in that but they still did not understand, I had to go to beat that old woman's words 'he won't be much good then' and to have my chance of revenge on Hitler.

Then one morning the sky seemed to be full of aircraft - all with three broad white bands around their wings and fuselage. It was D day, 6th June 1944, and on the twelfth I was eighteen - and received my call up letter.

Acknowledgements:

Thanks go to those who transformed my scruffy hand-written words into legible type and then into book form, initially my wife, Win, then both Nina Cox and Christine Haywood, and finally my daughter Ann.

Part two of My Life is in the process of being typed up – and I hope it will eventually become a book too.

Frank Samuel Foweraker
12th June 2016